TEACH YOU

BALLROOM
Dancing

BALLROOM
Dancing

THE IMPERIAL SOCIETY OF TEACHERS OF DANCING

Revised by Peggy Spencer MBE Fellow and Examiner of the
Imperial Society of Teachers of Dancing

TEACH YOURSELF BOOKS

For UK orders: please contact Bookpoint Ltd, 39 Milton Park, Abingdon, Oxon
OX14 4TD. Telephone: (44) 01235 400414, Fax: (44) 01235 400454. Lines are open
from 9.00 – 6.00, Monday to Saturday, with a 24 hour message answering service.
Email address: orders@bookpoint.co.uk

For U.S.A. & Canada orders: please contact NTC/Contemporary Publishing, 4255
West Touhy Avenue, Lincolnwood, Illinois 60646 – 1975 U.S.A. Telephone: (847) 679
5500, Fax: (847) 679 2494.

Long-renowned as the authoritative source for self-guided learning – with more than
30 million copies sold worldwide – the *Teach Yourself* series includes over 200 titles
in the fields of languages, crafts, hobbies, sports, and other leisure activities.

British Library Cataloguing in Publication Data
Imperial Society of Teachers of Dancing
   Ballroom Dancing. – 2 Rev. ed. – (Teach Yourself Series)
   I. Title   II. Spencer, Peggy   III. Series
   792.8

Library of Congress Catalog Card Number: 92-80858

First published in UK 1977 by Hodder Headline Plc, 338 Euston Road, London
NW1 3BH

First published in US 1992 by NTC/Contemporary Publishing, 4255 West Touhy
Avenue, Lincolnwood (Chicago), Illinois 60646 – 1975 U.S.A.

Printed in Great Britain for Hodder & Stoughton Educational, a division of Hodder
Headline Plc, 338 Euston Road, London NW1 3BH by Cox & Wyman Ltd, Reading,
Berkshire.

Impression number	19	18	17	16	15	14	13	12
Year		2004	2003	2002	2001			

———— CONTENTS ————

—— FOREWORD ——

William Cobbett said 'Dancing is at once rational and healthful. It is the natural amusement of young people and such it has been from the days of Moses'. Our only quarrel with this statement is the reference to 'young people', since the recreation of dancing provides pleasure and enjoyment, with relaxation and an improved social life, to people of all ages and all backgrounds. It is an ideal path to health through gentle exercise in these days of tension, stress and sedentary work and pleasures. Those who foresake the television screen to go dancing reap great mental and physical rewards.

It is to help everyone to enjoy these benefits that this book has been written on behalf of the Imperial Society of Teachers of Dancing, one of the world's leading societies, which through its eleven branches represents every aspect of the great Art of the Dance. The Ballroom Branch founded in 1924 developed and perfected what is known as the 'English Style'* of ballroom dancing which has become established throughout the world and especially in Australia, South Africa and Europe. In recent years the style has also been taken up extensively in Japan and the USA. Because of the worldwide spread of interest in this style of dancing, it is often now referred to as the 'International Style'.

The object has been to provide a book for the absolute beginner who wishes to dance socially and gain pleasure by knowing all the many rhythms and types of social dance which are used throughout the world while not being over-burdened with too advanced a description of any one of them. The beginner will benefit even more if he uses the book in conjunction with classes at his local school of ballroom dancing. Almost every school arranges beginners' classes, where many of the rhythms covered in this book are taught in easy stages with an excellent opportunity to practise to the latest records. All teachers put the beginner at his ease and show him that to learn dancing is fun and that everyone can soon enjoy it. In the UK the ISTD at Euston Hall, Birkenhead Street, London WC1H 8BE will advise generally and send the address of a local school of dancing to anyone who enquires. The addresses of linked overseas societies are listed at the back of the book.

Of course many thousands of people who begin as social dancers become keen to improve their standard, since in its advanced form ballroom dancing becomes a highly skilled and almost an athletic pastime. For the more skilled dancer, schools arrange medal classes at Bronze, Silver, Gold and higher levels in preparation for the amateur medal tests arranged by the ISTD. Similarly many dancers become keen to participate in the competitions that are arranged throughout the world and which cater for a wide range of dancing ability from the complete novice to the National Champion.

My final word is that dancing at any level of ability improves your health, enhances your social life and adds to your enjoyment of leisure, and the eminent teachers who wrote this book have many years of experience in teaching beginners to dance from which they hope you will benefit.

Victor Silvester
formerly President, ISTD

*Editor's Note:

English Style – Waltz, Foxtrot, Tango and Quickstep

In essence this was the dancing developed to American ragtime music and based on natural movement (walking steps) instead of Ballet as in the Old Time Waltz and Polka (on the toes with the feet turned out). The four dances evolved from a collaboration between the best ballroom dancers of the early Twenties in England. Five leading dancers – Josephine Bradley, Eve Tynegate-Smith, Muriel Simmons, Lisle Humphries and Victor Silvester were brought together by the Imperial Society in 1924 to form the original committee of the Ballroom Branch and to perfect, analyse, and standardise the dances and subsequently to examine intending teachers in the technique which the Committee established.

— INTRODUCTION —

This book is intended for the absolute beginner, whose interest has been aroused in dancing and who would like to tackle the job more intelligently than simply learning a series of mechanical motions that enable him, or her, to 'get round the floor'. The dances covered come into four categories: traditional ballroom dances, such as the Waltz; Latin-American dances, such as the Rumba, the Cha Cha Cha and the Mambo, Rock'n'Roll and Disco/Freestyle; and social and solo dances particularly suitable for all social occasions such as weddings, anniversaries, holidays or annual dances. No book can substitute for a good teacher but, where a teacher is not at hand, there is no reason why reasonable proficiency in the dances should not be attained by studying this book, provided that sufficient practice is put in to enable the steps and figures to be performed without conscious thinking. If, as is desirable, a dancing school is being attended, the book can act as an aide-mémoire of the teacher's instructions and make home practice easier. At a school, having made progress and developed an enthusiasm for the dances, the beginner may become keen to enter for one, or more, of the Society's 'Popular Dance Tests', which are not difficult and are great fun. They serve as an encouragement to go further because they mark progress in a tangible manner. The requirements for these tests are covered in this book.

1 How this book is arranged

Each dance, because of its special music, has a slightly different approach. It is essential therefore to study the notes preceding the actual steps before working on the dance.

When starting to study the foot positions, for instance in the Waltz, practise one small unit over and over again until the steps feel easy and natural, then work on the next three or four foot positions. Although the complete dance is written in one go, it is wise to try one unit at a time.

Dancing is based on natural walking steps forward and backwards. If this can be achieved with balance, control and small steps, the actual figures will feel and look natural and rhythmic. So it is best to study and work on the recommended exercises before working on the figures.

There is no specific order in which the dances should be performed or learnt. The Waltz, for instance, is used for weddings, anniversaries and often as the last dance at a function.

2 How to use this book

The important principle is to resist the temptation to try too much at one time. Many beginners, in sheer enthusiasm, want to learn every possible variation before they are able to dance the basic movements, smoothly and without effort, and with a true feeling for the music.

The best method is to select three dances – for example, the Social Foxtrot, Waltz and Cha Cha Cha, and master thoroughly the foot placements, the leg action, and the body and arm positions in the basic movement for each dance. Concentrate on the first figure or exercise described in the book for the particular dance, put on some suitable music and practise until you feel that what you are doing is expressing the rhythm and meaning of the music. Restrict yourself to three dances until you can do up to two figures in each without conscious effort; then go on to another dance if you feel so inclined but, once again, start by becoming completely at ease with the basic movement.

3 *Dressing for dancing*

This is a difficult question, with no single or specific answer. Like so many other social activities, it is important that the dress, whether of man or woman should conform. What you wear will depend on the company and the place in which the dance, or function, is held. One of the main attractions of the dances which are described in the book is the width of their field of practice; in other words, they may be danced at a dance centre or studio, a small and informal club, or at a State Ball. You would not go into a jazz club wearing white tie and tails and, similarly, you would not appear at the International Ballroom Championships wearing jeans.

When attending group classes, practice dances, or private lessons at a Dancing School or Studio, the generally accepted wear for men is a suit. In hot weather, jackets are removed and men wear designer-style shirts. However, nowadays nobody seems to object to more casual wear that can be more comfortable than suit, collar and tie. It is often wise to telephone for information on dress code before going to an event or club.

For women it is not so difficult to choose the most suitable dress for a particular function, because the fashion of the day will usually decide the issue. What is important, however, is that your dress or trouser suit is comfortable to dance in.

If dancing at hotels, restaurants or clubs, there can be regulations or restrictions which may be imposed by the management. There is no fixed rule and if you cannot find out what is required beforehand, it is best to dress in a way that you know will be acceptable. Shoes, of course, are *the* most important part of a dancer's equipment. They affect your appearance and your comfort; and your comfort affects your enjoyment of dancing. The same rules apply to men and women.

Some dancing venues like to protect their dance floors from outdoor shoes and expect you to wear shoes specially made for dancing. These are easily obtainable and will help you to improve your balance and control.

Never wear new shoes for dancing as they will almost certainly result in blisters; try them out at home first.

It is wise to go to considerable trouble to find a shoe, or have one made, that is broad enough, yet gives the support you need. For women,

'Court' shoes are most suitable for Ballroom dancing; open sandals with a 2½–3 inch (6–7 cm.) heel are usually best for Latin American. Whatever shoes you have, it is very important that the soles are light and *flexible*. Your feet, especially in dances such as the Rumba, have to *feel* the floor, to the extent that you virtually press the movement into the boards. It is also possible to buy shoes with non-slip soles, or you can stick on an oversole of soft chamois leather which has the same effect. But remember that the foot should be able to slide over the floor with a reasonable amount of freedom, so a completely non-slip sole will make dancing difficult.

For men, patent or glace kid shoes are no longer as popular as they were: calf or suede always look smart and comfortable.

4 At the dance

Remember that, no matter how good a dancer you are, it is bad taste to show off your steps regardless of others on the floor, and to impose them on your partner if she/he is not of the same standard. In fact, if you have not danced together before, it is advisable to keep to social dancing especially when in a crowded restaurant or club.

It is generally accepted that dances at social occasions such as weddings, holiday venues, small clubs and cruise events, require small steps and smart social type dancing.

People who dance as a hobby usually practise at dance clubs and competition practice nights.

5 Music

It is important to choose records, tapes or compact discs (CDs) that have been specially recorded for dancing and are therefore in the correct tempo for beginners. There is a varied selection of very high quality recordings readily available.

There are a number of specialist mail-order companies that supply records, cassettes and CDs for dancing.

If you are able to visit a large record store, look under Strict Tempo or

Dance bands. Try to find covers which clearly state the dance each track is for, (e.g. Charmaine . . Waltz). If this information is not given it is best to find a recording where each track is matched to a specific dance, unless you know what you are buying. (Suitable bands include Tony Evans, Ross Mitchell, Gunter Norris.)

As you progress and become more adventurous, try more authentic Latin recordings, or newly released music that you hear on the radio. These are often great fun to dance to.

HOW TO STUDY
DANCES AND
INDIVIDUAL FIGURES

First select the dance you want to concentrate on and get suitable music for it. Study very carefully the directions at the beginning of each dance where it is usually indicated that a basic movement or repetitive exercise is recommended to get the feel of the basic step or action. This is because the dance will be developed from that basic step or action, and it is essential to practise that first. When studying the figures in each dance, look carefully for turns or changes of body position with partner, particular in the Latin dances; often the change of position with a partner is the attractive variation of the basic theme. For instance, the New York in the Cha Cha Cha is in side-by-side position, not facing position. The time steps in the Cha Cha Cha are in Solo position. The Fallaway rock in the Jive commences in Fallaway position, so it is essential to understand these changes of body position to produce the correct effect of the figure being danced.

Foot positions alone do not make the figure complete; the rhythm, the correct position in relation to the room, the body position in relation to a partner and the study of arm and hand leads with a partner are all important parts of the figure. Very often the term **Small steps** is used. Take careful note of this, because a large step will cause bad balance and ugly leg lines and could be responsible for making the dancer out of time with the music. In any case, small steps for social dancing are a must. Popular ballrooms, clubs and dancing classes are usually quite crowded. Although you may learn to dance in an empty room with a teacher or a partner, keep in mind that your dancing must eventually take place on a crowded floor and so attention to direction, leading and consideration for others on the floor are essential ingredients to a happy evening of dancing.

The commencing and finishing positions given in each figure are given as a guide to assist the beginner. Eventually the figures must be adjusted to the amount of space available and the conditions in which the dancers find themselves. Try to study the musical value of each step (given under the heading **Timing** to the right of the man and the woman's steps – and applying to both) and the difference between a slow step and a quick. Dancing would not be such a joy if every step had the same beat value, and the challenge comes in understanding how to amalgamate the slows and quicks, and even (as in Jive and Cha Cha Cha) the faster type of chasse movement.

Good dancing relies considerably on the co-ordination of feet, body and arms, which takes a little time, so do not get impatient. Practice makes perfect.

―――――――― **Abbreviations used** ――――――――

L   Left

R   Right

LF   Left Foot

RF   Right Foot

LOD   Line of Dance

Q   Quick

S   Slow

&   and (denotes ½ beat)

a   a   (denotes ¼ beat)

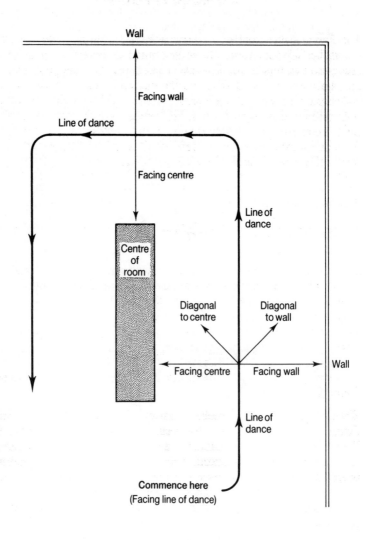

Line of dance

The line of dance represents an imaginary line drawn anti-clockwise round the Ballroom floor. The dancer who has driven on the right will recognise that this line of direction is on exactly the same principle; i.e. the outer wall of the Ballroom is the equivalent of the pavement and buildings on his *right*. To facilitate travelling round the Ballroom without collision it is necessary to try to keep progression anti-clockwise, wall on right, centre on left. For example, if the dancer travels across the Ballroom he will inevitably collide with those on the 'other side of the road'. This line of dance (LOD) is individual to each couple (*see Fig. p. 8*).

Alignments

Having understood the term LOD it can be seen that, if the dancer turns a quarter of a circle to the right from his LOD he will find himself *facing squarely to the outer wall of the Ballroom* an alignment known as *Facing Wall (FW)*. If he turns less, i.e. an eighth of a circle, he will be *facing diagonally to wall (DW)*. The same technique applies to Left or Reverse turns from facing LOD: after the dancer turns a quarter circle to the left he will find himself facing squarely to the centre of the Ballroom; if he turns less, i.e. an eighth of a circle to the left he will be *facing diagonally centre (DC)*.

The line of dance only applies to the travelling dances – Waltz, Social Foxtrot, Social Quickstep, The Quickstep, Quick Waltz, Samba, Paso Doble and the Tango. But don't be misled – most floors are crowded and travel is and should be limited. In the remaining dances there need be no progression round the room and alignments which relate to wall and centre of the room need not apply. However, in the descriptions of non-travelling dances it has been thought helpful to include commencing and guiding alignments.

Where only one alignment is given, this relates to the man.

Choreography

The figures given for each dance can be combined in different ways to give variation. Suitable figure combinations are suggested in the **Choreography** section at the end of each dance as a guide only.

How to interpret foot positions

The positioning of one foot is given in relation to the other, where there are no other instructions.

RF forward: forward in relation to LF, weight on RF.
RF side: to side in relation to LF, weight on RF.
RF diagonally forward: between a forward and side step in relation to LF, weight on RF.
LF back: back in relation to RF, weight on LF.
LF side: to side in relation to RF, weight on LF.
LF diagonally back: between a back and a side step in relation to kF, weight on LF.

This system applies in reverse when weight is held on RF. Where the term without weight but with pressure is used, this means that the foot is closed very firmly to the other foot but *without* transferring weight.

—— Holds and body positions ——

Ballroom holds

Fig. 1 Front view of man. Right arm round woman with his right hand just above her waist, and below her left shoulder-blade. His left arm is raised and bent at the elbow. Both elbows should be on a line just above waist level.

Fig. 2 Front view of the woman. Left arm resting lightly on man's forearm, near his shoulder, her hand with the fingers together. Her right hand is placed in his left hand and her head is looking over his right shoulder.

Fig. 3 Side view of hold without contact, sometimes preferred by the beginner. No change in the general outline, but the man and the woman will now be standing with feet about 6 in (15 cm) apart in relation to each other. Without body contact it is important for the man's arms to be especially firm in order to lead and guide the woman.

Fig. 4 Tango, front view. Man's right arm is further round woman causing her to stand slightly more to his right side. His left arm is in a more compact position. The weight is held firmly on RF with the right toe level with the left instep. Knees are slightly flexed but firm. Woman's left hand is placed on the man's back just below his shoulder.

Fig. 5 Promenade Position. Man facing front and travelling sideways. Characteristically a V-shape in which the woman is turned slightly to her right. Contact is retained on man's right side and woman's left side.

Fig. 6 Quickstep. Example of man's forward step taken outside woman on her right side. RF immediately in front of LF with the body slightly underturned in order to maintain contact with the woman.

Latin holds

Fig. 7 Open Facing Position. Facing and away from partner, man holding woman's right hand in his left hand, or with Double Hold.

Note: Normal Latin Hold or Closed Facing Position. Facing partner, slightly apart, with hold as shown in **Fig. 3** or with no hold or Double Hold (see **Fig. 9**). A slightly lower arm hold and more relaxed attitude is used for the Jive and Rock.

Fig. 8 Change of Places Right to Left. This position is used in Jive, and in the Alemana Turn in Rumba and Cha Cha Cha, when the woman is turning under raised arms.

Fig. 9 Double Hold. This hold is used in the Hand to Hand Rumba and Cha Cha Cha and in several figures in the Merengue, Lambada and Mambo.

Fig. 10 Promenade Position. As explained in **Fig. 5** but standing a little apart. Counter Promenade Position is also a V-shaped position with woman on man's left side maintaining normal hold. These positions are often used in the Latin dances.

Fig. 11 Fallaway Position. As Promenade Position but with man and woman moving backwards. This position is used in Jive, Merengue (Basic Fallaway), and Paso Doble (Ecarte), Lambada and Mambo.

Fig. 12 Change of hands behind Back.
This position is used in Jive and Rock,
etc.

Fig. 13 Left Side-by-Side Position.
Woman on man's left side, both facing
the same way. This hold is used in the
Cha Cha Cha, Rumba, Mambo, Jive and
Rock.
Note: The positions are reversed for
Right Side-by-Side Position, woman
being on man's right side.

Exercises

The demands and pressures of everyday life create many problems for the human body – leaning over an office desk, continuous standing in a shop, driving for hours on a motorway and so on.

To dance, especially with a partner, demands an upright poise, legs moving forward and backwards in correct alignment, arms held up lightly, head held high and shoulders kept down and relaxed. The following exercises, if rehearsed with care and dedication, will prepare the body, knees and legs for balanced and controlled dancing.

Play medium tempo music or disco tape music to help create an atmosphere:

Start with feet together, head held high, shoulders down and relaxed. Achieve a feeling of balance and feel a *centre* line from head to heels.

To relax the knees

Gently bounce both knees at the same level down and up, to music if possible (samba or disco music is helpful). The bounce action must be soft and continuous; use a little sing song: *bounce and bounce*.

To develop use of the balls of the feet

Begin with feet together, toes and heels, and body poised as in previous exercise.

Raise both heels from the floor putting a slight forward pressure into the balls of both feet. Gently lower both heels to the floor. Repeat to strengthen ankles and to make feet pliable. Use a little sing song: *rise and lower, rise and lower*.

Steps

Walking forward: (small steps)

Start with weight on LF:

RF fwd (nose and toes in line),
LF fwd (nose and toes in line),
RF fwd (nose and toes in line),
LF fwd (nose and toes in line).

Walking backward:

RF back,
LF back,
RF back,
LF back.

Sing song: *Forward 2 3 4, Back 2 3 4.*
Forward 2 3 4, Back 2 3 4.

Practise this over and over again to achieve a feeling of dance in the legs, hips and body. Keep knees relaxed and walk on two imaginary straight lines.

Side closes to right:

Start with weight on LF:

Place RF to side, small step.
Close LF to RF.
Place RF to side, small step.
Close LF to RF.

Side closes to left:

Start with weight on RF:

Place LF to side, small step.
Close RF to LF.
Place LF to side, small step.
Close RF to LF.

Repeat these two exercises many times to achieve a positive close of feet and change of weight. The two exercises can be combined, in which case Step 4 closes *without* weight:
Sing song: *Side 2 3 4, Side 2 3 4.*
Right 2 3 4, Left 2 3 4.

Work hard on this preparatory work.

BALLROOM
DANCES

1

—————— WALTZ ——————

When the Waltz was introduced into England during the early 19th century it scandalised society. Never before had the man clasped the lady to him in a facing position with his arm round her waist and rotated round the ballroom in what was almost an embrace; and rarely, if ever, had the dancers appeared to be dancing for their own pleasure as opposed to providing entertainment for admiring onlookers. Add to this the turned out toes derived from classical ballet which were still in use in the Ballrooms of that time and the impact must have been considerable. We hear much of the disapproval voiced by the older generation, but seldom mentioned is the fact that the reigning Queen (Victoria) was a keen and expert ballroom dancer with a special love of the Waltz.

Fortunately, the violent opposition faded out and the Waltz weathered an exciting and varied career, emerging today in two accepted forms, both reflecting the main characteristics of the dance. These are known respectively as the Modern (or Diagonal) Waltz and the Viennese (or Quick) Waltz.

It would be necessary to study a detailed history of ballroom dancing to follow the various changes that finally brought us the present-day version, but briefly it can be said that just before and during the First World War the Waltz went out of fashion in England, and a craze for the new syncopated rhythms brought over from America swept the country.

So although waltz music was still popular the tempo was slower and the steps had no set form. In the early 1920s, attempts were made by the teaching profession to find a uniform basic step that expressed this music, while at the same time following the accepted natural walking action. Finally, it was agreed that the feet should close on the third beat of a bar whether Forward Forward Close, or Forward Side Close. Right and Left Turns alternated by Change Steps were recommended, the man making a whole turn from the position at which he started, sometimes dancing as many as two or three complete Right and Left turns in sequence.

This style became the basis of the dance and, indeed, is the essence of the Waltz as described in this chapter. Over the years exponents have extended and developed the number of figures which are available to the dance but the elegant foundation remains.

——————————— The dance ———————————

Music

Time-signature 3/4, indicating three beats to a bar of music. The best music for this should have a strong melody, such as *The Last Waltz*, *Fascination* or *Charmaine*.

Balance

This can be defined as the ability of the dancer to maintain an upright and controlled position of the body whether in movement or still. This is especially important when rising on to the toes – as in the Forward and Backward Change steps and Turns. Many factors are involved in achieving good balance, but the first point to consider is the positioning of the arms and head, i.e. the hold.

Man's hold

Practise first *without* a partner. Stand with the feet together, toes pointing the same way (not turned out) and the knees straight but not stiff or rigid. Feel the weight of the body to be over the centre of the feet and test this by raising and lowering the heels in quick succession. The arms should be held down each side of the body with the palms facing straight forward. Now raise your arms so that they are at right angles to the body. (You will appear to be stopping two lanes of traffic.) Without moving head or shoulders bend your right arm at the elbow so that your right hand is facing slightly above the centre point of your waist. Now bend your left elbow and raise your hand *upwards* to finish in a position about level with your head. Walk about the room in this position and begin to imagine that your right arm is the one that is *round* the woman and your left hand holding her right hand. (The effect is rather as if the man has created a protective 'frame' round her so that he can control the movements they are going to do together, and prevent others from banging into them.)

Woman's hold

The woman responds to the man's initiative by placing her left arm so that her hand rests comfortably, but *not* heavily, near his shoulder, light pressure in her fingers creating a sense of security but without weight. He will hold her right hand in his left, preferably without the palms touching. She should stand very slightly to his right side, and in this position she can keep her head nicely poised and looking over his right shoulder. It is very upsetting to the balance of the partnership if the woman continually moves her head from one position to another – even if conversing!

Having secured a comfortable yet secure 'hold', the task of the woman is now two-fold. She must follow the man's lead at all times – including his mistakes! She must also remember that he is a partner and *not* a porter! In effect she must carry her own weight and in this way learn the art of balance.

Footwork

An important factor in achieving good balance is the correct use of the different parts of the foot. Although it is a fair comparison to liken the action of the feet to that of walking, it must at the same time be realised that in the latter the moving foot is lifted before being placed on the floor. As one of the beauties of this style of dancing lies in its continuity and smoothness of movement, it must be understood that this can only be achieved if some part of the moving foot remains in light contact with the floor throughout.

To clarify this we will describe the footwork of the 'Closed Change', forward and backward, and this method can also be applied to the Right and Left Turns.

Right and Left Turns are self-explanatory terms which help beginners to grasp the basic steps. The professional terms, however, are **Natural** – meaning to the right – and **Reverse** – meaning to the left: hence, Natural and Reverse Turns.

_____ Right Foot Closed Change _____ (Forward)

Man

Start with the feet together, weight on LF. Move the RF forward with pressure on the whole of the front part of the foot. As the foot advances, release the heel of the back foot (this helps to transfer the weight forward). To complete the stride, use the right heel as in a normal walk, taking the weight well over the whole foot.

During this action the heel of the back foot (left) is further released so that the ball of the foot can be drawn up a little towards the RF before moving into a sideways position (**Step 1**).

Now place the LF to the side on the ball of the foot and release the right heel (**Step 2**).

With the sensation of pressing upwards from the ball of the RF and the weight almost entirely over the LF, close RF to LF taking the weight on the RF, feet together on toes of both feet (**Step 3**).

Now lower the right heel in preparation for the next figure.

Woman

Stand with feet together, weight on RF. Move LF back with pressure at first on the ball of the foot; as the foot continues to move back it will stretch out to the toe. At the extent of the stride the pressure will be transferred to the ball of the foot and later the front toe released (this takes the weight to a central position) (**Step 1**).

Draw the RF back and at the same time lower the left heel. Then step to the side on the ball of RF, releasing the left heel (**Step 2**).

With the sensation of pressing upwards from the ball of the LF and the weight almost over the RF, close LF to RF taking the weight entirely on the LF as LF closes to RF. Feet together on toes of both feet (**Step 3**).

Now lower left heel in preparation for the next figure.

Note: It is understood that at first beginners may wish only to 'Walk' through the pattern of the figures to music, but the more advanced footwork has been given in some detail so that they may later enjoy the genuine spirit of the Waltz with its attractive *rise and fall*. For a better understanding of this it will be necessary – as the pupil progresses – to master the natural knee action, flexing on lowering steps and straightening on rising steps. Use a practise sing song: *forward side close, forward side close*, and repeat.

Figures

1 Right Foot Closed Change

Precede with Right Turn.

	Man Commence facing diagonally centre, weight on LF:	**Woman** Commence backing diagonally centre, weight on RF:	**Timing**
1	RF forward	LF back	1
2	LF side	RF side	2
3	RF closes to LF	LF closes to RF	3

Follow with Left Turn, below.

2 Left Foot Closed Change

Precede with Left Turn.

	Man Commence facing diagonally wall, weight on RF:	**Woman** Commence backing diagonally wall, weight on LF:	**Timing**
1	LF forward	RF back	1
2	RF side	LF side	2
3	LF closes to RF	RF closes to LF	3

Follow with Right Turn, below.

For the purpose of practice, Closed Changes can be danced in sequence forwards and backwards, commenced facing LOD.

3   *Right Turn*

Precede with LF Closed Change.

	Man	**Woman**	**Timing**
	Commence facing diagonally wall, weight on LF:	Commence backing diagonally wall, weight on RF:	
1	RF forward facing diagonally wall, commencing to turn right	LF back diagonally wall commencing to turn right	1
2	LF side, continuing turn, backing diagonally centre	RF side, continuing turn, right toe pointing down LOD (see Note)	2
3	RF closes to LF backing LOD	LF closes to RF facing LOD	3
4	LF back, commencing to turn right	RF forward, commencing to turn right	1
5	RF to side, right toe pointing diagonally centre, body facing centre	LF side, continuing turn, backing centre	2
6	LF closes to RF facing diagonally centre	RF closes to LF backing diagonally centre	6

Note: To avoid blocking the Man's forward movement the woman should move her right leg back before placing the RF sideways for Step 2. This figure creates a *box* shape. When the steps have all been understood, gradually turn to the Right until the idea of turning is easier.

Follow with RF Closed Change

4 Left Turn

Precede with RF Closed Change.

	Man	Woman	Timing
	Commence facing diagonally centre, weight on RF:	Commence backing diagonally centre, weight on LF:	
1	LF forward facing diagonally centre, commencing to turn left	RF back backing diagonally centre, commencing to turn left	1
2	RF side, continuing turn, backing diagonally wall	LF side, toe pointing to LOD continuing to turn left (see Note) (body turns a quarter of a turn)	2
3	LF closes to RF, continuing to turn backing LOD	RF closes to LF facing LOD	3
4	RF back, commencing to turn left	LF forward, commencing to turn left	1
5	LF to side, body facing wall	RF side, continuing turn, backing wall	2
6	RF closes to LF facing diagonally wall	LF closes to RF continuing turn, backing diagonally wall	3

Note: To avoid blocking the man on Step 2 the woman should move the left leg back before placing the LF sideways. The Left Turn also creates a *box* shape. Use the practice sing song: *forward side close, back side close*, and repeat it.

Follow with LF Closed Change.

5   *Hesitation Change*

Precede with first three steps of Right Turn.

	Man Commence backing LOD weight on RF:	**Woman** Commencing facing LOD weight on LF:	**Timing**
4	LF back, commencing to turn right, backing LOD	RF forward commencing to turn right	1
5	Turning on left heel, RF to side, facing diagonally centre	LF side, continuing to turn, backing diagonally centre	2
6	With weight on RF draw LF slightly towards RF facing diagonally centre. Retain weight on RF (Hesitate)	With weight on LF close RF to LF without changing weight (Hesitate) backing diagonally centre	3

Follow with Left Turn.

6   *Waltz Quarter Turn*

Precede with LF Closed Change.

	Man Commence facing diagonally wall, weight on LF:	**Woman** Commence backing diagonally wall, weight on RF:	**Timing**
1	RF forward, commencing to turn right	LF back, commencing to turn right	1
2	LF side continuing turn, facing wall	RF side, continuing turn	2

	Man	**Woman**	**Timing**
3	RF closes to LF continuing turn, backing diagonally centre	LF closes to RF, facing diagonally centre	3
4	LF back, backing diagonally centre	RF forward, facing diagonally centre	1
5	RF side, backing diagonally centre	LF side, facing diagonally centre	2
6	LF closes to RF, backing diagonally centre	RF closes to LF, facing diagonally centre	3
7	RF back, commencing to turn left	LF forward, commencing to turn left	1
8	LF side, body facing wall	RF side, continuing turn, backing wall	2
9	RF closes to LF, facing diagonally wall	LF closes to RF backing diagonally wall	3

Follow with LF Closed Change.

7 *Right Spin Turn*

Precede with LF Closed Change.

	Man	**Woman**	**Timing**
	Commence facing diagonally wall, weight on LF:	Commence backing diagonally wall, weight on RF:	
1	RF fwd commencing to turn right	LF back, commencing to turn right	1
2	LF side continuing to turn	RF side continuing turn	2
3	RF closes to LF completing ⅜ of a turn to end backing LOD	LF closes to RF, facing LOD	3

WALTZ

	Man	Woman	Timing
4	LF back a small step, spin a ½ turn on LF to end facing LOD	RF fwd a small step, spin a ½ turn on RF to end backing LOD	1
5	RF fwd between partner's feet continuing to turn	LF to the side and slightly back	2
6	LF to side and slightly back (take care not to drop weight backwards)	RF diagonally fwd almost between partner's feet	3

Note: See the Quickstep Right Spin Turn on page 57 for more on this step.

Choreography

(a) LF Closed Change.
    Waltz Quarter Turns.

(b) LF Closed Change.
    Right Turn.
    RF Closed Change.
    Left Turn.

(c) LF Closed Change.
    Right Spin Turn.
    Steps 4, 5, 6 Left Turn.

(d) 1–3 Right Turn.
    Hesitation Change.
    Left Turn.
    LF Closed Change.

2

SOCIAL FOXTROT (SLOW RHYTHM)

The social foxtrot has evolved from that very subtle and flowing dance, known the world over simply as the Foxtrot. At its best, the Foxtrot is a very individual dance, and perhaps the most characteristic of the original English Style, the very casual effect masking a strength of action and a far from casual response to its rhythm. Although the name was not recognised until just after the First World War and the dance not standardised until many years later, the idea behind it had been germinating in America for quite a time, together with a great many other dances created in response to the *new beat*. It is still not very clear how the 'fox' came into it, but what is clear is that just before the First World War New York was buzzing with excitement over a fantastic dance called the **Foxtrot**.

In the meteoric rise to fame of the Vernon Castles, exhibition dancers of outstanding talent and charm, there was no doubt at all that the Foxtrot was the most original and exciting of their various dances. They walked, tripped, skipped and generally moved around the floor in perfect unison, mostly in ballroom hold, and richly deserved the thunderous applause they received.

The élite of the dancing world were soon trying to capture the unusual style of movement and when a very talented American, G. K. Anderson, came over to London, and with Josephine Bradley won many competitions, he set the seal – so to speak – on the style of the Foxtrot. Miss Bradley was not only a beautiful dancer with crystal-clear movement, but she had a unique flair for teaching, and there is no doubt the world fame of the Foxtrot owes much to her brilliance.

However, because of the great popularity which ballroom dancing was enjoying, it was necessary to evolve a form of dance that could express the slow syncopated 4/4 rhythm and yet remain 'on the spot'. This did not mean that the 'travelling' foxtrot was dropped – far from it – but the 'on the spot' dance did provide a means of enjoying the music in a background which large numbers of people could afford and enjoy, and where various bands, big and small, were all producing excellent and individual musicians and experimenting with and perfecting all the new sounds and beats from America.

At first this 'on place' dancing was known appropriately as *crush*, then *rhythm* dancing. It is now called 'social' and possibly this best conveys its purpose and its limitations.

This may be clearer to understand if approached from the negative point of view: it would be anti-social to attempt to stride round a ballroom crowded with dancers, to dance with only one partner when out with a party, or to be so engrossed with the performance of figures that any conversation is taboo. Moreover, it can create a very good base – should it be desired – for the Foxtrot.   (P.H.)

-------------------- **The dance** --------------------

Music

Time signature 4/4, indicating four beats to a bar of music. For descriptive purposes the timing of the steps is given in Slows and Quicks. A Slow represents two beats or '1 2' (or '3 4'); a Quick represents one beat or '1' or '2' or '3' or '4'. Recommended tempo: 30 bars per minute.

Hold

This is described fully in the Waltz section, but in very crowded conditions it should be made as compact as is comfortable, somewhat resembling the Tango. In the early phases of learning, 'close contact' is not essential provided that the arms are firm and stylish so as to look pleasant and to lead and follow without difficulty.

Footwork and balance

In this dance, the leg and foot action is the same as in a normal walk, the weight being carried over the forward foot, but not being allowed to drop back when moving backwards.

Unlike the Waltz where there is an elevation on to the toes on the closing steps, in Social Foxtrot all the side steps, though taken on the ball of the foot, are lowered on to the heel as the feet close.

While it is necessary and correct to learn the figures on a 'walking basis', unless the knees, feet and body react to the music, and particularly the rhythm, obviously the effect and feeling will be rather lifeless and dull. In fact it will not be dancing, so although there are many different ways of interpreting rhythm and music there are certain factors that can act as extra guide-lines to the beginner. These will follow the formal descriptions when necessary.

—————————— Figures ——————————

1 Quarter Turn

Steps 1–4: Quarter Turn to Right: Steps 5–8: Quarter Turn to Left.

Man	**Woman**	**Timing**
Commence facing diagonally wall, weight on RF:	Commence backing diagonally wall, weight on LF:	
1 LF forward	RF back	S

	Man	**Woman**	**Timing**
2	RF forward, commencing to turn right	LF back, commencing to turn right	S
3	Continuing turn, LF side facing wall	Continuing turn right, RF side small step, toe pointing diagonally centre	Q
4	Continuing turn very slightly RF closes to LF, backing diagonally centre, weight on RF	Turning body slightly right, LF closes to RF, weight on LF facing diagonally centre	Q
5	LF back	RF forward	S
6	RF back, commencing to turn left	LF forward, commencing to turn left	S
7	Continuing turn left, LF side small step, toe pointing diagonally wall	Continuing turn left, RF side backing wall	Q
8	Turning body slightly left, RF closes to LF, weight on RF facing diagonally wall	Turning left, close LF to RF weight on LF, backing diagonally wall	Q

2 *Right Pivot Turn*

	Man	**Woman**	**Timing**
	Commence backing diagonally centre, weight on RF:	Commence facing diagonally centre, weight on LF:	
1	LF back small step, very slightly leftwards commencing to turn right	RF forward between partner's feet, commencing to turn right	S

	Man	**Woman**	**Timing**
2	Take weight forward to RF continuing turn	Continuing turn, LF back and very slightly leftwards	S
3	Continuing turn right, LF side	Still turning, RF small step side	Q
4	Still turning, close RF to LF, weight on RF, having turned just over a quarter turn right	Continuing turn, close LF to RF weight on LF, having made just over a quarter turn to right	Q

Note: The man may find it useful to know that the above Right Rock Turn, if repeated three times from the alignment given, constitutes a complete turn, so that he will end where he began – backing diagonally centre. At a corner, twice complete is adequate and can be followed by the Quarter Turn to left or the Back Corté down the new LOD.

When learning figures that are danced 'on the spot' or 'in place' it can help beginners to achieve a satisfactory performance if the man marks out the steps, before taking a partner. He will notice that although the first step 'LF back' should be thought of as 'back', it will tend to be slightly leftwards with the toe turned very slightly inwards. This happens because he has already started to turn his body to the right, which also gives the woman the necessary lead.

His next step 'RF forward' should remain 'on the spot', but the foot will be replaced turned slightly rightwards in order to follow the turn of the body to the right.

The third step 'LF side' should now move up towards the RF before stepping to the side, and as the RF closes to LF there is a slight swivel on the ball of the LF to complete the turn. The whole weight is now on the RF.

By keeping the steps fairly small, the man will not run the risk of upsetting his balance or that of his partner, and if all the above is going well he will find that the inside of his right knee will come in light contact with his partner's on the second step.

The woman should have no difficulty in following this figure, the continual rotary feeling of the movement acting as a guide to which she can respond.

3 Left Pivot Turn

	Man	Woman	Timing
	Commence facing diagonally wall, weight on RF:	Commence backing diagonally wall, weight on LF:	
1	LF forward, commencing to turn left	RF back, commencing to turn left	S
2	Transfer weight back to RF continuing to turn left	Transfer weight forward to LF continuing to turn left	S
3	Still turning, LF side small step, toe pointing diagonally centre	Still turning, RF to side	Q
4	Turning body slightly left, RF closes to LF, weight on RF, facing diagonally centre	Turning to left, close LF to RF weight on LF, backing diagonally centre	Q

The left Pivot can be repeated four times complete and followed by the Quarter Turn to Right.

The most important point for the man in this figure is for him not to carry his weight too fully over the first step 'LF forward', as this might mislead the woman into thinking he intends to continue travelling forward, instead of which he is in fact going to 'check back' on to his RF. Because of this checking action, the left turn must be deliberate but gentle in action, allowing the weight to be comfortably over second step (RF back) which is replaced almost 'in place' except for a slight inward turn of the foot in order to synchronise with the turning of the body to left.

The third step 'LF side' should first be drawn towards the RF before stepping to the side, the heel of the RF now being released, so as to immediately close to the LF. The weight is now firmly on the RF with the heel lowered.

Once having initiated this continuous turn to left, it is very easy to repeat the figure – say, four times in all – but it is necessary to be sure about which figure is to follow, so that the woman can sense the change in the lead.

4   Back Corté

	Man	Woman	Timing
	Commence backing diagonally centre, weight on RF:	Commence facing diagonally centre, weight on LF:	
1	LF back	RF forward	S
2	RF back	LF forward	S
3	LF to side	RF side	Q
4	RF closes to LF, weight on RF, end backing diagonally centre	LF closes to RF, weight on LF, end facing diagonally centre	Q

Follow with Quarter Turn Left.

5   Side Step (Balance to Left and Right)

	Man	Woman	Timing
	Dance Quarter Turn to Right, but end facing wall, weight on RF	Dance Quarter Turn to Right, but end facing centre, weight on LF	SS QQ
1	LF side, RF closes towards LF, keeping weight on LF	RF side, LF closes towards RF, keeping weight on RF	S
2	Move RF slightly sideways against LOD. LF closes towards RF, keeping weight on RF	Move LF slightly sideways against LOD. Close RF towards LF, keeping weight on LF	S

	Man	**Woman**	**Timing**
3	LF small step sideways	RF small step sideways	Q
4	RF closes to LF weight on RF	LF closes to RF weight on LF	Q

This figure can be repeated two or three times. To conclude, turn slightly to right on Steps 3 and 4 so as to end backing diagonally centre. Follow with Quarter Turn to Left. This figure travels sideways progressively along LOD, man's body facing wall, woman's backing wall.

6 Promenade Walk and Chasse (Conversation Piece)

Entry to Promenade Walk and Chasse.

	Man	**Woman**	**Timing**
	Commence facing diagonally wall, weight on RF:	Commence facing diagonally centre, weight on LF:	
1	LF forward	RF back	S
2	RF forward preparing to lead partner to Promenade Position	LF back commencing to turn right (preparing for Promenade Position)	S
3	LF side in Promenade Position	RF side in Promenade Position facing diagonally centre	Q
4	RF closes to LF in Promenade Position, weight on RF	LF closes to RF in Promenade Position, weight on LF	Q

Promenade Walk and Chasse:

	Man	**Woman**	**Timing**
1	LF to side in Promenade Position, along LOD pointing diagonally wall	RF side in Promenade Position, along LOD pointing diagonally centre	S

Man	**Woman**	**Timing**
2	RF forward and across LF in Promenade Position	LF forward and across RF in Promenade Position	S
3	LF small step to side in Promenade Position	RF small step side in Promenade Position	Q
4	RF closes to LF in Promenade Position, weight on RF facing diagonally wall	LF closes to RF in Promenade Position, weight on LF	Q

This figure can be repeated two or three times. To conclude: the man turns slightly to right to end square with partner, backing diagonally centre. Now follow with Quarter Turn to left.

———— Choreography ————

(a) Quarter Turn right.
Quarter Turn left.
Quarter Turn right.
Three Right Pivot Turns.
Quarter Turn left.

(b) Quarter Turn right.
Quarter Turn left.
Four Left Pivot Turns.
Quarter Turn right.
Back Corté.
Quarter Turn left.

(c) Quarter Turn right.
Three Right Pivot Turns.
Back Corté.
Quarter Turn left (end facing wall).
Three Side Steps (Balance left and right).
Quarter Turn left.

3
SOCIAL QUICKSTEP (QUICK RHYTHM)

A great many people, especially students, wrongly assume that the Social Quickstep preceded the development of the orthodox Quickstep but, as with the Social Foxtrot, this was not the case and this seems a good opportunity to explain what really happened.

Imagine the period as about the early 1930s when the really enthusiastic dancers had their own favourite, exclusive (and expensive) dance clubs, where they were able to move freely and where so much that is now taken for granted as the 'English Style' originally came into being.

The beginner would visit the few well-known teachers and after private lessons 'graduate' to the tea dance or weekly evening dance. There was also much entertaining by important society hostesses in their own ballrooms where dancing played a very important part, especially for the débutantes.

Against this background the question of *social* dancing did not arise. *Ballroom* dancing was enjoyed by a small group and, judging by today's nostalgia for the period, everyone seems to have enjoyed themselves very much indeed.

However, as economic difficulties arose, this background faded out; now it was the turn of the very popular Palais de Danse to take over not only the enthusiasts, but a completely new public who of course needed a new approach. Much effort has been made to *codify* what this approach should be but only comparatively recently has it been given the attention it deserves; without strenuous effort this simple 'walking' variation of the Quickstep can be adapted to almost any tempo and danced with confidence in any part of the world. (P.H.)

The dance

Music

Time signature 4/4, indicating four beats to one bar of music. For descriptive purposes the timing of the figure is given in Slows and Quicks: 'Slow' represents two beats – *One, Two* or *Three, Four*; 'Quick' represents one beat – *One* or *Two* or *Three* or *Four*. Tempo recommended is 52 bars per minute.

Hold, balance and footwork

Basically the same as in Social Foxtrot but, due to the increased speed of the music, the steps will tend to be shorter and the heel-leads less pronounced. There are many different ways of expressing rhythm through the body, knees and feet, but perhaps the most unattractive style is the use of the arms (known as Pump-handling). One rhythmic interpretation which can be introduced is a Charleston action; this is simple to learn, always fashionable and can be applied as the dancer feels inspired.

A description of this and a method of practice are given at the end of this section.

Figures

1 Quarter Turn

Steps 1–4: Quarter Turn to Right. Steps 5–8: Quarter Turn to Left.

	Man	**Woman**	**Timing**
	Commence facing diagonally wall, weight on RF:	Commence backing diagonally wall, weight on LF:	
1	LF forward	RF back	S
2	RF forward, commencing to turn right	LF back, commencing to turn right	S
3	Continuing turn, LF small step to side, facing wall	Still turning, RF side, small step	Q
4	Still turning slightly, RF almost closes to LF, backing diagonally centre, weight on RF	LF almost closes to RF facing diagonally centre, weight on LF	Q
5	LF back	RF forward	S
6	RF back, commencing to turn left	LF forward, commencing to turn left	S
7	Draw LF back to end with left heel closing to right heel. Toe pointing diagonally wall	Continuing to turn left, RF to side, backing wall	Q
8	Turning body to left, close RF to LF facing diagonally wall, weight on RF	Still turning, LF closes to RF backing diagonally wall, weight on LF	Q

2   *Right (Natural) Pivot Turn*

In this figure the pattern, number of steps and alignment are exactly the same as in the Social Foxtrot (see page 37). On account of the faster music it is not necessary to close the feet completely on the fourth step.

3   *Left (Reverse) Pivot Turn*

For this figure also the number of steps and pattern are the same as in the Social Foxtrot (see page 39).

On account of the speed of the music the action of the feet on Steps 3 and 4 are identical to Steps 3 and 4 of the Quarter Turn to left.

4   *Back Corté*

	Man	**Woman**	**Timing**
	Preceded by Quarter Turn to right. Commence backing diagonally centre, weight on RF:	Preceded by Quarter Turn to right. Commence facing diagonally centre, weight on LF:	
1	LF back	RF forward	S
2	RF back	LF forward	S
3	LF small step to side	RF to side	Q
4	RF almost closes to LF, end backing diagonally centre, weight on RF	LF almost closes to RF, end facing diagonally centre, weight on LF	Q
	Follow with Quarter Turn to left	Follow with Quarter Turn to left	

5   Side Step

Precede with Quarter Turn to left. Man facing wall, weight on RF.

	Man Commence facing wall, weight on RF:	**Woman** Commence facing centre, weight on LF:	**Timing**
1	LF to side	RF to side	S
2	Close RF to LF	LF closes to RF	S
3	LF very small step to side	RF very small step to side	Q
4	Close RF to LF	LF closes to RF	Q

Note: Dance three times, turning slightly to right between third and fourth steps of third side step. End backing diagonally centre. Follow with Quarter Turn left.

———————— Choreography ————————

(a) Quarter Turn to right, Quarter Turn to left, end facing diagonally wall.
     Quarter Turn to right, end backing diagonally centre.
     Four Right Pivot Turns, end backing diagonally centre.
     Quarter Turn to left, end facing diagonally wall.

(b) Quarter Turn right, Quarter Turn left, end facing wall.
     Side Step. Dance three times, end backing diagonally centre.
     Quarter Turn to left.

(c) Quarter Turn right.
     Back Corté.
     Quarter Turn to left.
     Quarter Turn to right.
     Quarter Turn to left, end facing wall.
     Three Side Steps, end backing diagonally centre.
     Quarter Turn to left.
     Three Left Pivot Turns, end facing diagonally wall.

The Charleston Lilt

Moving Forward:

> Stand with feet together, arms in Ballroom Hold or held easily at sides, weight on RF, facing LOD:

1   Step forward on to LF, knee straight, body slightly braced; leave right toe in place behind LF (*Count 1 or Quick*)
    Now flex left knee slightly, RF still in place (*Count 2 or Quick*);

2   Step smartly forward on to RF, knee straight, body slightly braced, left toe in place behind RF (*Count 3 or Quick*).
    Flex right knee slightly, left toe still in place (*Count 4 or Quick*).

Practise moving forward until it feels quite natural.

Moving Backward:

> Stand with feet together, weight on LF, backing LOD:

1   Step back on to RF, taking weight over the foot, but keeping front LF in place (*Count 1 or Quick*).
    Now flex right knee slightly, keeping LF still in place (*Count 2 or Quick*);

2   Step smartly back on to LF, keeping RF in place, knee straight, body slightly braced (*Count 2 or Quick*).
    Flex left knee very slightly, keeping RF in place (*Count 4 or Quick*).

These movements should be practised to music, without a partner at first and preferably at home, moving backwards and forwards until the action feels natural, after which it should be possible to introduce this action into the figures of the dance.

——— QUICKSTEP ———

The history of this dance is difficult to trace because, unlike most other ballroom dances that are now universally popular, it was not directly inspired by the sudden emergence of a new 'beat' or rhythm or of a particular kind of music coming from abroad, nor were there any stage or screen personalities exhibiting it when it first evolved.

By about 1926 the farmyard collection – Bunny-Hug, Turkey Trot and others – had all lost favour, leaving the Foxtrot, Waltz, Tango and One-step (originally invented by the Vernon Castles, but to different music), as the required dances for entry to championships.

It is with this One-step that we are concerned, because there is no doubt that it instilled in the dancers of that period certain qualities which were to become an integral part of the English style in general, and of the Quickstep at certain times in its career. Two of these essential qualities were that the man's forward and backward steps must be in 'straight alignment' with the woman's together with a continuity of progress created by a firm swing of the leg from the hip while gliding lightly round the floor in the manner of a walk (i.e. heel-leading). Lively and smart when well done to the rather martial type of music (Valencia was a firm favourite), it can be seen that these essentials were good training for the future.

At this time great changes were taking place in dance bands and dance music; new and more exciting tunes were being produced, young people had the opportunity to improvise and practise at home to records and the 'Big Bands' in the hands of famous leaders were providing Jazz and Beat music which had great popular appeal.

So it was that the music of the One-step with its lack of syncopation gradually faded out; the music died and the dance died with it. The bands with the help of radio literally 'called the tune' and the dancers had to follow, thus creating for themselves a new interpretation of Foxtrot to suit music now played very much faster.

Then came the Charleston explosion. An off-beat dance of extraordinary vitality, the Charleston combines a flexing and stretching of the knees with an in-and-out twisting of the feet and a contra swing of the arms, if danced without a partner. It is extremely exciting to do and to watch. Ballroom floors everywhere became a flailing mass of arms and legs, but not for long. PCQ (**Please Charleston Quietly**) and **No Kicking Please** boards were soon produced and rules strictly enforced, and so the Charleston faded and died, although it left a very vivid impression on the young and gifted dancers of the day.

The *Star* Championship (promoted by the newspaper of that name) had already in 1927 replaced the One-step with the Quick-time Foxtrot and Charleston. Following upon this the Imperial Society, with *The Dancing Times* decided to organise the British Professional Championship and also to eliminate the One-step, and replace it with *The Quickstep* (thus getting rid of a descriptive, but very cumbersome name).

The overall Championship was taken by Maxwell Stewart and Pat Sykes, but the Quickstep section was won by Alec Miller and Phyllis Haylor, who without a vestige of kicking had managed to convey the charm of the Charleston, together with other very simple little figures including the Millar Cross (now called Cross Swivel) all fitting easily into the *new* music. This competition put the Quickstep firmly on the map, and it has been one of the standard four English Style dances ever since. (P.H.)

The dance

Various important points must be mastered to help to produce an enjoyable performance of the Quickstep, as distinct from the Social Quickstep.

Contact with partner

As this is really the cornerstone or the beauty of the original English style, expressed ideally as *two people moving as one*, it is vital to grasp that this effect can only be arrived at if it is clear that one or other of the partnership is moving either on the *outside* or the *inside* of parts of a circle that almost invariably make up the pattern (or figures) of the dances.

For instance, in the first part of the Right Turn in the Waltz the man moves forward and round the woman and is therefore on the outside of the *arc* (or part of a circle), while on the last part – Steps 4, 5, 6 – he is on the inner rim of the arc. The right interpretation of this idea throws light on what may appear to be complicated points of technique.

Timing and construction of figures

The Social Quickstep can be expressed as 'Slow, Slow, Quick, Quick' danced in varying directions. In the Quickstep, the *Right Foot Forward*, although starting as a **Walk** (technically known as a heel-lead), really acts as a springboard to prepare the man for the rise on to the ball of his foot for the following Chasse (a shorthand term for three steps indicating Side, Close, Side), in this instance danced on the balls of his feet. Then, following the first four steps of the Quarter Turn he can either dance the Heel-Pivot which keeps him *in-line* with the woman and is a most useful and clever little movement for the dancer to learn (see page 45, Steps 6, 7, 8), or the alternative, which is the Progressive Chasse. This is perhaps the most characteristic figure of the dance and one which well rewards a close study of the notes because it finishes in a foot position *outside* the partner, but still in contact with her, of course.

It is in the execution of this figure in particular that the dancer may find it worth while to refer back to the opening theme regarding the artistic aspect of *contact* and how best to approach this, as obviously it is not always easy to recognise this *principle*. Other adjustments connected with these ideas are included in the descriptions of the figures.

Do not be discouraged by the exaggerated way in which the Quickstep is danced in competitions. With so much talent around, all this exaggeration is a pity and certainly unnecessary, but until the spectator becomes more discerning and the surrounding atmosphere less commercial, it appears to be unavoidable.

The best thing for the beginner to do is to observe and enjoy, but not imitate, and then to approach his own study of the Quickstep slowly.

Music

Time signature 4/4, indicating four beats to one bar of music. For descriptive purposes the timing of the figures is given in Slows and Quicks: **Slow** represents two beats: *One, Two* or *Three, Four*; 'Quick' represents one beat: *One* or *Two*; *Three* or *Four*. Tempo recommended is 50 bars to the minute. The hold is as for the Waltz.

Figures

1 Quarter Turn to Right

	Man	Woman	Timing
	Commence facing diagonally wall, weight on LF:	Commence backing diagonally wall, weight on RF:	
1	RF forward, commencing to turn right, rising from heel-lead to ball of foot as second step moves into position	LF back, commencing to turn right. Ball of foot to heel	
			S

	Man	**Woman**	**Timing**
2	LF to side, continuing to turn to face wall. LF placed on ball of foot	RF to side pointing diagonally centre, continuing turn, body facing centre. RF placed on ball of foot	Q
3	Continuing turn on ball of LF, close RF to LF on ball of foot. Backing diagonally centre, weight on RF	Continuing to turn slightly in body, close LF to RF, ball of foot. Facing diagonally centre, weight on LF	Q
4	Move LF sideways backing diagonally centre (no further turn). Ball of foot lowering to heel as next step is taken	RF diagonally forward (slightly between partner's feet) facing diagonally centre. Ball of foot lowering to heel as next step is taken	S

2 *Progressive Chasse*

Precede with Quarter Turn to Right.

	Man	**Woman**	**Timing**
	Commence backing diagonally centre, weight on LF:	Commence facing diagonally centre, weight on RF:	
1	RF back, commencing to turn left, ball of foot to heel	LF fwd, commencing to turn left. Heel-lead to ball of foot	S
2	LF to side, pointing diagonally wall, body facing wall. Ball of foot	Continuing to turn, RF to side backing wall, ball of foot	Q

	Man	**Woman**	**Timing**
3	Slight body turn to left, RF closes to LF, body almost facing diagonally wall, feet facing diagonally wall, ball of RF	Continuing turn on ball of RF, close LF to RF on ball of foot. End body almost backing diagonally wall, feet backing diagonally wall, weight on LF	Q
4	Move LF sideways and slightly forward in relation to RF preparing to step outside partner. Ball of foot lowering as next step (5) is taken	Move RF sideways, backing diagonally wall. End RF side and slightly back in relation to LF. Ball of foot lowering to heel as next step (5) is taken	S
5	RF forward outside partner, facing diagonally wall, body almost facing diagonally wall. Heel-lead to whole foot	LF back, partner outside. Backing diagonally wall, body almost backing diagonally wall	S

Note: Follow with Forward Lock Step or Right (Natural) Pivot Turn, Right (Natural) Spin Turn using the last step of the Progressive Chasse as the first step of the next figure.

3 Forward Lock Step

Precede with Progressive Chasse.

	Man	Woman	Timing
	Commence facing diagonally wall (body almost facing diagonally wall), weight on LF:	Commence backing diagonally wall, body almost backing diagonally wall, weight on RF:	
1	RF forward outside partner. Heel-lead preparing to rise to ball of foot	LF back, man outside. Ball, heel LF	S
2	LF diagonally forward, ball of foot	RF back	Q
3	RF crosses behind LF, weight on RF, ball of foot	LF crosses in front of RF, ball of foot, weight on LF	Q
4	Travelling diagonally wall, LF diagonally forward, ball of foot lowering to heel as next step (5) is taken	RF diagonally back, ball of foot lowering to heel as next step (5) is taken	S
5	RF forward outside partner. Heel-lead to whole foot	LF back	S

Note: This figure travels in a diagonal line to wall.

Follow with Right Turn or Right Spin Turn outside lady on right side. (Step 5 becomes Step 1 of the Right Turn.)

Follow with Quarter Turn to Right. See also **Choreography**.

4   *Right (Natural) Pivot Turn (round corner)*

Precede with the Progressive Chasse.

	Man Commence facing diagonally wall, weight on LF:	**Woman** Commence backing diagonally wall, weight on RF:	**Timing**
1	RF forward, outside partner commencing to turn right, rising from heel-lead to ball of foot as second step (LF) moves into position	LF back, commencing to turn right. Ball of foot to heel	S
2	LF to side, continuing turn to back diagonally centre. LF placed on ball of foot	RF to side, continuing to turn, pointing to LOD. Place on ball of foot	Q
3	Continuing turn on ball of LF, close RF to LF on ball of foot, lowering right heel as next step (4) is taken. Weight on RF, backing LOD	Continuing turn, close LF to RF. Ball of foot lowering to heel as next step (4) is taken. Facing LOD, weight on LF	Q
4	LF back and very slightly leftwards. Turn to right on ball of LF allowing left heel to touch the floor. Hold RF forward in direct line with LF as turn is made, then release left heel. End with weight on ball of LF, facing diagonally wall of new LOD	RF forward facing LOD heel-lead. Turn to right on ball of foot holding LF back. Lower heel of RF as turn is completed. End backing diagonally wall of new LOD	S

Man	Woman	Timing
Take weight forward to RF making this the first step of Quarter Turn to Right.	Take weight back to LF for first step of following figure.	

5 Right (Natural) Spin Turn

Precede with Forward Lock Step.

	Man	Woman	Timing
	Commence facing diagonally wall, weight on LF:	Commence backing diagonally wall, weight on RF:	
1	RF fwd commencing to turn right outside woman	LF back, commencing to turn right	S
2	LF side continuing turn	RF side continuing turn	Q
3	RF closes to LF completing ⅜ of a turn to end backing LOD	LF closes to RF, facing LOD	Q
4	LF back a small step, spin a ½ turn on LF to end facing LOD	RF fwd a small step, spin a ½ turn on RF to end backing LOD	S
5	RF fwd between partner's feet continuing to turn	LF back and slightly to Left still turning. RF brushes LF without weight. RF diagonally fwd (slightly between partner's feet)	S
6	LF to side and slightly back (take care not to drop weight backwards)		S

Continue with RF back into Progressive Chasse.

To understand this figure, think of it in three parts:

Steps 1–3	the turn to Right
Step 4	the Pivot
Steps 5 and 6	the Spin

A helpful reminder is the line: *Turn Q Q, Pivot, Spin, Chasse.*

This figure has also been used in other dances such as the Waltz and the Social Foxtrot by adapting to the timing of the particular dance.

Choreography

(a)   Quarter Turn to Right.
Progressive Chasse.
Forward Lock Step.
Natural Spin Turn.
Progressive Chasse.

5

—— QUICK WALTZ ——

During almost the whole of Queen Victoria's reign, the 'Quick' or Viennese Waltz remained popular and this continued well into the 20th century, in fact until the arrival of the 'new sound' (American jazz syncopation).

This sustained popularity of the 'Quick' Waltz was assured by the extraordinary amount of good music composed in its idiom: first Weber (1786–1826) with his *Invitation to the Waltz,* in which Nijinski gave an inspired and electrifying performance in Monte Carlo in 1911; then Chopin (1810–1849), whose waltz music forms the background of *Les Sylphides,* thus creating a vehicle for Margot Fonteyn – as well as other great artists including Anna Pavlova. There are the musical shows too, such as *The Merry Widow* whose musical score by Franz Lehàr (1870–1948) included a waltz of universal popularity and is still performed; these are just a few of the outstanding examples of the music available.

The dance itself is known to have been created and danced by the peasantry of Southern Germany and Bavaria as early as 1780. It was called *The Ländler* and its chief characteristic was the continuous and swift rotations and turning figures danced by the man and his partner. This was the dance that arrived in Vienna and eventually came into its own, for in the 19th century Johann Strauss and his son, also called Johann, managed between them to write hundreds of 'quick-time' waltzes, Johann Junior being responsible for the opera *Die Fledermaus* and *The Blue Danube*. The dance now became known as the *Viennese Waltz* and was danced by everyone, not only the peasantry – whether in Vienna, Paris, London or New York.

Although today the quick-time waltz is played less often than in the past, a study of the dance is useful. 'Party' and Sequence Dances very often include a few bars of waltzing (usually played at rather less than 'top' speed). Here is some advice on how to begin the practice:

1   Keep all the steps small and rather 'flat'; this may sound strange, but it makes for steadiness and timing when dancing at speed.

2   Remember that the accent is on the first beat: find this and let it 'carry you through' the bar. (Conductors vary in the interpretations, which can be confusing if you are trying to count 1–2–3 and work out figures at the same time). All the 'hesitations' are particularly useful in this respect.

The *Viennese Waltz* proper is beyond the scope of this book, but the Quick Waltz will provide a foundation for further study in the technique should the beginner wish to improve his standard and become a more advanced dancer.   (P.H.)

The dance

Music

Time signature: 3/4. Tempo: approx 60 bars per minute.

Hold

Contact, as in the Waltz, which facilitates the rotating action of two or more Right (Natural) or Left (Reverse) Turns when they are danced continuously.

Footwork

In view of the speed of the music the dancer does not rise high on to his toes.

———— Figures ————

Side Hesitation

For Preliminary Practice:

	Man Commence facing LOD, weight on LF:	**Woman** Commence backing LOD, weight on RF:	**Timing**
1	RF side, releasing left heel	LF side, releasing right heel	1
2	Rising very slightly on ball of RF, close LF towards RF keeping weight on RF	Rising slightly onto ball of LF, close RF towards LF, keeping weight on LF	2
3	Hesitate with weight on RF lowering right heel at end of 3rd beat	Hesitate with weight on LF, lowering left heel at end of 3rd beat	3
4	LF to side, releasing right heel	RF side, releasing left heel	1
5	Rising very slightly on to ball of LF, close RF towards LF keeping weight on LF	Rising very slightly on to ball of RF close LF towards RF keeping weight on RF	2
6	Hesitate with weight on LF, lowering left heel at end of 3rd beat	Hesitate with weight on RF, lowering right heel at end of 3rd beat	3

The above is a preliminary practice action for the beginner to become accustomed to the quick tempo, and can be repeated as desired.

1   *Right (Natural) Turn*

Precede with LF Change Step.

	Man	**Woman**	**Timing**
	Commence facing diagonally wall, weight on LF:	Commence backing diagonally wall, weight on RF:	
1	RF forward, commencing to turn right. Heel, ball	LF back, commencing to turn right. Ball, heel	1
2	LF side, continuing turn, backing diagonally centre. Ball of LF	RF side, pointing LOD. Ball of foot	2
3	Continuing turn on LF, RF closes to LF. End backing LOD, weight on RF. Ball, heel	Continuing turn, LF closes to RF. End facing LOD, weight on LF. Ball, heel	3
4	LF back and slightly leftwards, commencing to turn right. Ball, heel	RF forward, commencing to turn right. Heel, ball	1
5	RF small step side, pointing diagonally centre. Ball of foot	LF side, continuing turn. Backing centre. Ball of foot	2
6	LF closes to RF, facing diagonally centre. Weight on LF. Ball, heel	RF closes to LF, backing diagonally centre. Weight on RF. Ball heel	3

Follow with RF Change Step (see page 64).

Note: The alignments are given as a guide only, fewer turns can be made, if desired, but always finish in an anti-clockwise direction.

2 Left (Reverse) Turn

Precede with RF Change Step.

	Man	Woman	Timing
	Commence facing diagonally centre, weight on RF:	Commence backing diagonally centre, weight on LF:	
1	LF forward, commencing to turn left. Heel, ball	RF back, commencing to turn left. Ball, heel	1
2	RF side and slightly back, continuing turn. Backing diagonally wall. Ball of foot	Continuing turn, LF small step to side, pointing to LOD. Ball of foot	2
3	Continuing turn, LF crosses in front of RF. Backing LOD, weight on LF. Ball, heel	Continuing turn, close RF to LF facing LOD. Weight on RF. Ball of foot, lowering heel at end of step	3
4	RF back, commencing to turn left. Ball, heel	LF forward, commencing to turn left. Heel, ball	1
5	Continuing turn, LF small step side, pointing diagonally wall. Ball of foot	RF side and slightly back, continuing turn. Ball of foot	2
6	RF closes to LF continuing turn. End facing diagonally wall, weight on RF. Ball of foot lowering to heel at end of step	Continuing turn, LF *crosses* in front of RF. End backing diagonally wall, weight on LF. Ball, heel	3

Follow with LF Change Step.

3 *Change Step*

Left Foot Change Step: precede with Left Turn.

	Man Commence facing diagonally wall, weight on RF:	**Woman** Commencing backing diagonally wall, weight on LF:	**Timing**
1	LF forward, Heel, ball	RF back. Ball, heel	1
2	RF diagonally forward, ball of foot	LF diagonally back, ball of foot	2
3	LF closes to RF. End facing diagonally wall weight on LF. Ball, heel	RF closes to LF, weight on RF. Backing diagonally wall. Ball, heel	3

Follow with a Right Turn. This Change Step can also be curved slightly to the left.

Right Foot Change Step: precede with Right Turn.

	Man Commence facing diagonally centre, weight on LF:	**Woman** Commence backing diagonally centre, weight on RF:	**Timing**
1	RF forward, heel, ball	LF back, ball, heel	1
2	LF diagonally forward, ball of foot	RF diagonally back. Ball of foot	2
3	RF closes to LF facing diagonally to centre. Weight on RF. Ball, heel	LF closes to RF backing diagonally to centre. Weight on LF. Ball, heel	3

Note: This step can also be curved slightly to the right.

Follow with Left Turn.

4 *Forward and Backward Hesitation*

	Man	**Woman**	**Timing**
	Commence facing diagonally wall, weight on LF:	Commence with weight on RF:	
1	RF forward, heel lead	LF back, ball, heel	1
2	Release right heel, rising very slightly onto ball of RF. Close LF to RF, keeping weight on RF	Draw RF to LF, keeping weight on LF	2
3	Hesitate with weight on ball of RF, lowering right heel at end of 3rd beat as LF starts to move back	Hesitate with weight on ball of LF	3
4	LF back, ball, heel	RF forward, heel lead. Release right heel, rising very slightly on to ball of RF	1
5	Draw RF to LF, keeping weight on LF	Close LF to RF, keeping weight on RF	2
6	Hesitate with weight on ball of LF	Hesitate with weight on ball of RF lowering right heel at end of 3rd beat as LF starts to move back	3

These Forward and Backward Hesitations can be repeated without turn or turning gradually to the right. Practise as an 8-bar phrase. Exactly the same figure can be commenced with the left foot forward and right foot back either with or without turning left.

5 Scissors

Precede with the Left Turn.

	Man Commence facing diagonally wall, weight on RF:	**Woman** Commencing backing diagonally wall, weight on LF:	**Timing**
1	LF forward, commence to turn left. Heel, ball	RF back, commence to turn left. Ball, heel	1
2	Continuing to turn left, RF to side. Ball of foot	Continuing to turn. LF to side. Ball of foot	2
3	Continuing to turn on ball of RF almost close to LF to RF. Prepare to step outside partner. End facing diagonally centre, weight on LF. Ball, heel	Slight turn to left on ball of LF, RF closes towards LF, backing diagonally centre. Ball, heel	3
4	RF forward moving to centre, outside partner, commencing to turn right. Heel, ball	LF back, commencing to turn right. Ball, heel	1
5	Continuing to turn, LF to side, ball of foot	Continuing to turn, RF to side. Ball of foot	2
6	Turning to right on ball of LF, almost close RF to LF. Ball, heel. End facing diagonally wall, weight on RF, preparing to step to left side of partner	Turning to right on ball of RF, LF almost closes to RF. Ball, heel. End backing diagonally wall, weight on LF	3
7	LF forward to left side of woman, commencing to turn left. Heel, ball	RF back, commencing to turn left. Ball, heel	1

Man	**Woman**	**Timing**
8	Continuing to turn, RF to side. Ball of foot	LF to side. Ball of foot	2
9	Turning on ball of RF almost close LF to RF preparing to step outside partner. Ball, heel. End facing diagonally centre or diagonally wall of new LOD	Slight turn to left on ball of LF, RF almost closes to LF, weight on RF. End backing diagonally centre or diagonally wall of new LOD	3

Follow with Right Turn commenced outside woman or Forward Hesitation commenced outside partner.

Choreography

(a) Commencing facing diagonally wall,
    RF Forward and Backward Hesitation. Right Turn.
    RF Change Step.
    Left Turn. LF Change Step.
    These can be repeated.

(b) Commence facing diagonally centre,
    LF Forward Hesitation.
    RF Backward Hesitation turning left.
    LF Forward Hesitation.
    RF Backward Hesitation turning left.
    LF Forward Hesitation, end backing diagonally centre,
        (Man will have turned approximately half a turn).
    Steps 4, 5 and 6 of Left Turn, end facing LOD.
    Left Turn, end facing diagonally wall.
    LF Change Step.

(c)   Commence facing diagonally centre,
      RF Change Step.
      Left Turn, end diagonally wall,
      The Scissors, end diagonally centre.
      Right Turn, commenced outside partner, diagonally centre. (If danced round corner the Right Turn would commence diagonally wall.)

6

── TANGO ──

The Tango has been described as romantic, dramatic, exotic, sophisticated, simple and absurd and it may come as a surprise to the beginner
that a dance lending itself so readily to exaggeration and often appearing
so complicated, should be included as part of his basic repertoire. But it
has a long history, with periods of great popularity, and an individuality
and fascination which merit its inclusion. The Tango in dance form was
created by the Gauchos – those brilliant horsemen who were natives of
La Plato Pampas on the east coast of Argentina. The dance rhythm came
out of the highly rhythmic and melodious music played to them as they
rested in their saloons and taverns. It is characterised by an emphatic 2/4
time-signature and played with an unusual staccato accent on each beat.
So great was its popularity that later – just before the First World War –
the dance was banned in Argentina. Apparently it had lost its native
simplicity and become too uninhibited!

The veto was successful and the Tango reappeared in Paris, particularly
in restaurants and night clubs. The style was described as sensuous and
sophisticated and many admired the authentic atmosphere created by an
influx of guitarists and native orchestras. Its popularity soon spread to
England and Tango Teas were given wherever it was possible to find
the space. The Savoy Hotel was one of the first to introduce these and

hired some excellent musicians. Exhibitions were given in the theatres and dance clubs and the teachers of the period arranged their programmes to include this exciting new dance.

With the declaration of war in 1914 however, its popularity waned and it was not until some time later that Tango competitions were occasionally included in important events and presented at theatres.

In 1921 a film entitled *The Four Horsemen of the Apocalypse* brought the romantic and very photogenic Rudolph Valentino to everyone's notice, especially his dancing of the Tango. In spite of the great impact of his performance, the general public did not feel inspired to imitate him and the dancing profession itself was at this time very involved with the development of all the other rhythms and dances coming from America. Some leading teachers, however, were wise enough to visit Paris and continue their study of the Tango, rightly feeling that the dance should somehow be kept alive in England, and so it was that when the first examinations were organised, it was the Parisian style that was standardised. It certainly had much to offer, being quiet and sophisticated, but it was difficult to teach to the average pupil, and only real enthusiasts took it seriously.

This was the situation in the mid-1930s when a new interpretation was presented by a German competitive couple appearing in London for the first time. By emphasising the staccato effect, speeding up the music and slightly lengthening the stride, the dance took on a new life and everyone agreed that while still retaining its special character, here was a dance that looked stylish and should be possible to teach. This assessment proved to be correct and before long this Tango was being danced by the competitors and taught in the studios.

It must be admitted however, that it took a long time to arrive at a clear analysis of its unusual technique and even now there is not complete agreement about this. The tempo at which the music is played is also a point upon which there is disagreement, but this certainly need not deter the beginner. Different interpretations are a very definite characteristic and perhaps part of the magic of the Tango. (P.H.)

The dance

Music

The time signature of 2/4 indicates two beats to one bar of music. For descriptive purposes the timing of the figures is given in Slows and Quicks: a Slow represents one beat; and a Quick represents half a beat. *One and,* or *Two and,* equals *Slow,* while *One* or *and* or *Two* or *and* equal *Quick.* Tempo: approximately 33 bars to the minute.

Hold, balance and footwork

Although many different interpretations have appeared, at no time have these deviated from the theme of a partnership in which the man is dominant.

With this idea in mind we can understand the need for a closer hold than in the Waltz; in effect, the man places his right arm further round the woman and – to balance this picture – closes his left forearm slightly inwards (see Fig. 4). This closer hold, apart from creating a more compact appearance, will inevitably bring the woman slightly to his right side. Another effect of this hold is that when walking forward the right side of the body appears to take the lead and the step taken with the right foot will be a little *open* in position, with the right foot angled slightly leftwards to the line of travel.

To harmonise with the above the left foot is also angled leftwards in a direct line in front of the supporting right foot – matching the line of the body. A very common fault is to place the left foot **across** the line of the right foot thus overlocking the thighs; this distorts the body line and of course restricts movement.

Woman – hold and balance

If the man has taken up the position already described for him, the woman will find that he will hold her right hand a little more closely, with her forearm drawn inwards and facing downwards. Her left arm will now tend to be further round her partner and a little lower than in Waltz or Quickstep. Her left hand can then be placed under his left shoulder blade, with her fingers held together, slight pressure on the thumb and first finger and the palm facing downwards. The head and shoulders should be nicely poised as in other 'contact' dances.

Forward Walk

Stand with the body in the position described in the hold with the feet together. Now slip the right foot a few inches back so that the right toe is level with the left instep; this will help to hold the knees in a slightly flexed but very **firm** position.

With weight on the stationary foot (RF), place the LF forward – first on to the heel, then the whole foot, as in a normal walk. The heel of the back foot (RF) is now released, but some pressure is maintained on the ball of the foot which is still in contact with the floor, although the weight of the body is almost entirely over the forward foot. Count *One and* or *Slow*.

As the weight is transferred fully over the front foot (LF) the back foot moves up with the toe skimming the floor lightly, then as it approaches the forward foot, it will be lifted and placed forward first on the heel, then the whole of the foot. Count *Two and* or *Slow*.

Backward Walk

In contrast to the Forward Walk, the important point to remember is that the weight must not be taken too quickly over the foot stepping back.

Stand with the body in Tango hold and with feet together. Now slip the left foot forward a few inches so that the left heel is level with the right instep. The knees are now slightly flexed but firm.

With weight on the stationary left foot, place the right foot back on the ball of the foot, then release the toe of the front foot keeping slight pressure on the heel. The weight is now moving towards the back foot (RF). Count *One and* or *Slow*.

Taking the weight entirely over the back foot (RF) lift the front foot slightly and place it sharply back, releasing the toe of the right foot; the right heel lowers just before the left foot passes, thus making a second walk with the left foot. Count *Two and* or *Slow*.

The instructions in the **Hold, balance and footwork** may appear complicated, but study them carefully for without doubt they will, if understood, add considerably to the pleasure of performing the dance.

Figures

The figures have been chosen to fulfil the needs of a beginner attempting this dance for the first time.

1 Walks into Closed Promenade Position

	Man	**Woman**	**Timing**
	Preceded by Forward Walk on LF facing diagonally wall. Commence facing diagonally wall, weight on LF:	Preceded by Backward Walk on RF backing diagonally wall. Commence backing diagonally wall, weight on RF:	S
	RF forward, preparing to lead woman into Promenade Position	LF back	Q
	Turning body slightly, right, tap LF to side of RF, small step, keeping weight on RF, at same time leading woman to turn slightly to her right to Promenade Position:	With slight turn to right on LF tap RF to side of LF, small step keeping weight on LF. End in Promenade Position facing diagonally centre:	Q
1	LF to side in Promenade Position along LOD, LF pointing diagonally wall	RF to side in Promenade Position along LOD, RF pointing diagonally centre	S

	Man	Woman	Timing
2	RF draws towards LF and is then placed forward and across LF in Promenade Position	LF draws towards RF and is then placed forward and across in Promenade Position, commencing to turn body left	Q
3	LF side and slightly forward, leading woman to turn to left	Continuing to turn, RF side and slightly back, backing diagonally wall	Q
4	Turning body to left, RF closes to LF slightly back, weight now on RF End facing diagonally wall in line with woman	Continuing body turn, close LF to RF slightly forward, weight now on LF End backing diagonally wall in line with man	S

2 Rock Turn

	Man	Woman	Timing
	Commence facing diagonally wall, weight on RF, LF forward (One Walk):	Commence backing diagonally wall, weight on LF, RF back (One Walk):	S
1	RF forward, commencing to turn right	LF back, commencing to turn right	S
2	LF side and slightly back, backing centre	Move RF slightly rightwards between man's feet, taking weight on to it	Q
3	Transfer weight forward on to RF between woman's feet	Move LF slightly leftwards, taking weight on to it	Q

	Man	Woman	Timing
4	Very small step back LF	RF very small step forward	S
5	RF back to centre, turning slightly left	LF forward to centre, commencing to turn left	Q
6	LF to side, left toe turned slightly to left, body facing wall	RF side and slightly back continuing turn, backing diagonally wall	Q
7	Turning body to left, RF closes to LF slightly back, weight now on RF. End facing diagonally wall	Continuing body turn, close LF to RF slightly forward, weight now on LF. End backing diagonally wall	S

Note: The beginner can repeat this Walk and Rock Turn continuously round the ballroom for practice.

3 Open Left (Reverse) Turn Closed Finish

Precede with two Walks LF RF.

	Man	Woman	Timing
	Commence facing diagonally centre, weight on RF:	Commence backing diagonally centre, weight on LF:	S
1	LF forward, commencing to turn left	RF back, commencing to turn left	Q
2	RF side and slightly back, continuing turn backing LOD	Continuing turn, LF closes to RF, LF pointing down LOD releasing right heel	Q
3	LF back, backing LOD	RF forward, facing LOD	S
4	RF back, commencing to turn left	LF forward, commencing to turn left	Q

	Man	**Woman**	**Timing**
5	Continuing to turn left, LF sideways, left toe pointing slightly leftwards, body facing wall	Continuing turn, RF side and slightly back, backing diagonally wall	Q
6	Turning body to left, RF closes to LF slightly back, weight on RF, facing diagonally wall	LF closes to RF slightly forward, weight on LF, backing diagonally wall	S
	Follow with Walk forward on LF	Follow with Walk backward on RF	

Description of Promenade Position

This picture deviates from the normal situation of the man travelling forwards and the woman backwards, and vice versa. In effect the body-line of the couple is V-shaped with only the man's right side and the woman's left side in contact (Fig. 5).

———— Choreography ————

(a) One Walk on LF.
     Rock Turn, repeated round the ballroom (see page 74).

(b) One Walk on LF.
     Rock Turn, end facing LOD.
     Two Walks LF RF Turning slightly to Left.
Open Left (Reverse) Turn.
One Walk into Closed Promenade.

(c) One Walk.
     Rock Turn.
     Walk Into Closed Promenade.
     Two Walks Turning to Left.
     Open Left (Reverse) Turn.
     One Walk Rock Turn to start routine again.

LATIN-AMERICAN DANCES

7

—————— RUMBA ——————

Today the Rumba, as danced in the social ballroom or in competitions, is fairly well standardised and uniform in pattern. But this does not mean that the Rumba has always been a distinct and clearly categorised dance; in fact, its origin and evolution is a complicated story.

The word rumba is really a generic term, covering a variety of names, of which Afro-Cuban, Son, Son-Montuno, Danzon, Guajira, Mambo, Conga, Guaracha, Nanigo, are but a few. The names of the dances come from many sources, and one must not attempt any literal translations: For instance, **son** in Spanish simply means *sound*.

There are two sources of the dances: one Spanish, the other African. Although the main growth was in Cuba, there were similar dance developments which took place in the other Caribbean islands and in Latin America generally. The 'rumba influence' came in the 16th century with the black slaves imported from Africa. The dance was inspired by the walk of the cock and hence showed a similarity to the Chilean national folk dance – the 'Cueca'. In its first, primitive form, it rather scandalised the whites, and therefore underwent a refining process over the years. It was danced to a syncopated rhythm which *attacked* on the *second* beat of the music.

In Spain, the Bolero was a very old dance, which became considerably modified in its incorporation into the Cuban dancing. It became known as the Criollabolero (Criolla = Creole). Today, you can hear talk of the Rumba, the Son and the Bolero, without the users of these terms having much idea as to how they came about.

The dances are all rhythmically similar but vary considerably in tempo. In Latin America and the USA the Rumba is a fast dance, the Son of medium tempo, and the Bolero slow.

Between 1920 and 1950 the Cuban dance-halls were invaded by American-type jazz and boogie-woogie. It is clear that the American-type syncopation was assimilated into the rhythms of the Rumba, creating new and hybrid forms of Cuban jazz.

Basically the Rumba is the spirit and soul of Latin-American music and dance: it has completely fascinating rhythms and bodily expressions which enable the woman dancer to express her grace and femininity and the man to show her off in this way while himself feeling the spell of the music and the sheer joy of being alive.

Whatever its origin, and however it evolved, the Rumba as it is danced in ballrooms today in most countries around the world, is enjoyable, rhythmic, attractive and easy to learn.

In Europe, the introduction of Latin-American dancing – and the Rumba in particular – owed much to the enthusiasm and interpretative ability of Monsieur Pierre, who became London's leading teacher in this dance form.

Pierre was a Basque, and a skilled ballroom dancer and teacher. In the 1930s, with his partner, Doris Lavelle, he demonstrated and popularised Latin-American dancing in London. Up to the mid-1940s the accepted Rumba was that evolved and practised in the USA – the 'Square Rumba'.

Pierre and Lavelle introduced the true 'Cuban Rumba', danced on the second beat, but this was not accepted without much argument and was only finally established, through Pierre's efforts, as the officially recognised version, in 1955.

Today this Rumba has been developed for television and for national and international competitions. To make it interesting it has taken shapes and patterns from other dances, but its basic pattern of steps remains the same.   (G.W.)

The dance

Music

This is written in 4/4 time, 4 beats to a bar of music, and each beat should be given its full value – one for the first step, one for the second step and two for the third step. The tempo is 27–31 bars per minutes, the slower tempo being popular as it gives more time to *feel* the rhythm and to dance without effort.

Footwork, hold and action

The basic action of the Rumba should be a soft flexing and straightening of the knees, with a rhythmical hip movement. It is not a difficult dance to learn, once the basic rhythm is understood. The rhythm should be expressed through the feet, legs and hips, without any tendency to exaggeration.

Each step is taken on the ball of the foot with a flexed knee: when weight is taken on to the foot the heel lowers and the knee straightens: the heel of the other foot is now released and the knee is flexed. At this point the hips move gently to the side of the straightened leg.

The stance is erect without stiffness, the partners' bodies being well balanced, standing facing each other about 6 in (15 cm) apart. The man should hold the woman's right hand with his left at shoulder level, with her fingers between his thumb and first finger. His right hand is placed high on the woman's shoulder blade, and her left hand rests lightly on his right upper arm.

Alignments are given purely for ease in learning. As the Rumba is a non-progressive dance, the figures may be commenced and finished in any alignment.

The first step of the Basic Movement – left foot forward – is taken on the second beat in the Cuban Rumba. It is found to be easier if, to commence the dance, one takes a step to the side on the right foot and moves the hips gently to the right on the first beat.

Figures

1 Basic Movement

Commence in Normal Hold, feet apart or closed.

	Man Facing wall; weight on RF:	**Woman** Facing centre; weight on LF:	**Timing**
1	LF forward	RF back	2
2	Replace weight to RF	Replace weight to LF	3
3	LF to side and slightly back	RF to side	4 1
4	RF back	LF forward	2
5	Replace weight to LF	Replace weight to RF	3
6	RF to side	LF to side and slightly back	4 1

A gradual turn to the Left is made throughout. May also be danced without turn. May be repeated.

2 Side Step

Commence in Normal Hold, feet apart or closed. Precede with Basic Movement.

	Man Facing wall. Weight on RF:	**Woman** Facing centre. Weight on LF:	**Timing**
1	LF to side	RF to side	2
2	Close RF to LF	Close LF to RF	3
3–6	Repeat steps 1 and 2 twice LRLR	Repeat steps 1 and 2 twice RLRL	4 1, 2 3 4 1

May be danced without turn or with a gradual turn to left in a circular pattern. Follow with Basic Movement or Cucarachas.

3 Right Top (Turn to Right)

Commence in Normal Hold, feet apart. Precede with 1–3 of the Basic Movement without turn.

	Man	Woman	Timing
	Facing LOD. Weight on LF:	Backing LOD. Weight on RF:	
1	RF behind LF, toe to heel, toe turned out, commencing to turn to Right	LF to side, commencing to turn to Right	2
2	LF to side. Continuing to turn to Right	RF in front of LF, toe turned out, continuing to turn to Right	3
3	Close RF to LF	LF to side	4 1

Follow with Basic Movement or Side Step.

4 Cucarachas to Left and Right

(a) Side Cucaracha to Left

Commence in Normal Hold. Precede with Side Step.

	Man	Woman	Timing
	Facing wall: weight on RF:	Facing centre: weight on LF:	
1	LF to side with part weight	RF to side with part weight	2
2	Replace weight to RF	Replace weight to LF	3
3	LF closes to RF	RF closes to LF	4 1

Follow with Side Cucaracha to Right. **Note:** Step 1 may be danced diagonally back.

(b) Side Cucaracha to Right

Commence in Normal Hold. Precede with Side Cucaracha to Left.

	Man Facing wall: weight on LF:	**Woman** Facing centre, weight on RF:	**Timing**
1	RF to side with part weight	LF to side with part weight	2
2	Replace weight to LF	Replace weight to RF	3
3	RF closes to LF	LF closes to RF	4 1

Follow with Basic Movement. **Note:** Step 1 may be danced diagonally back.

5 Progressive Walk Forward and Backward

These are steps danced in groups of three or six, taken forward or backward. Forward Walks normally commence after 1–6 of the Basic Movement, stepping forward on RF on Step 6. Woman LF back. Backward Walks commence after 1–3 of the Basic Movement, stepping back on LF on Step 3. Woman RF forward. Follow Forward Walks with Basic Movement and Backward Walks with 4–6 of Basic Movement.

6 Side Rock

Commence in Normal Hold. Precede with 1–3 of Basic Movement.

	Man Facing LOD. Weight on LF:	**Woman** Backing LOD. Weight on RF:	**Timing**
1	RF to side	LF to side	2
2	Replace weight to LF	Replace weight to RF	3
3	Replace weight to RF	Replace weight to LF	4 1

Follow with New York or Basic Movement.

7 *Shoulder to Shoulder*

Commence in Normal Hold with feet apart. Precede with Basic Movement.

	Man	**Woman**	**Timing**
	Facing diagonally wall. Weight on RF, slightly forward, preparing to step outside partner on Left side:	Backing diagonally wall. Weight on LF:	
1	LF forward outside partner on Left side	RF back	2
2	Replace weight to RF	Replace weight to LF outside partner on Left side	3
3	LF to side and slightly forward, turning ¼ to Left	RF to side and slightly back, turning ¼ to Left	4 1
4	RF forward outside partner	LF back	2
5	Replace weight to LF	Replace weight to RF outside partner	3
6	RF to side and slightly forward, turning ¼ to Right	LF to side and slightly back, turning ¼ to Right	4 1
7–12	Steps 1–6 may be repeated, turning square to partner on last step		2 3 4 1 2 3 4 1

Follow with Side Step or Basic Movement.

8 New York

Commence in Normal Hold, feet apart. Precede with Side Rock or Basic Movement.

	Man	**Woman**	**Timing**
	Facing LOD. Weight on RF:	Backing LOD. Weight on LF:	
1	LF forward in Left Side-by-side position, turning ¼ to the Right, releasing hold with right hand	RF forward, turning ¼ to Left, releasing left hand	2
2	Replace weight to RF	Replace weight to LF	3
3	LF to side, turning ¼ to Left, taking partner's left hand in right hand and releasing hold with left hand	RF to side, turning ¼ to Right, releasing right hand	4 1
4	RF forward in Right Side-by-side position, turning ¼ to Left	LF forward, turning ¼ to Right	2
5	Replace weight to LF	Replace weight to RF	3
6	RF to side, turning ¼ to Right, taking partner's right hand in left hand and releasing hold with right hand	LF to side, turning ¼ to Left, releasing left hand	4 1
	Finish facing LOD	Finish backing LOD	
	Steps 1–6 may be repeated		

Note: Less turn may be made to take step 1 in Counter Promenade Position and step 4 in Promenade Position.

Follow with Basic Movement or Alternative Basic Movement.

9 *Woman's Under Arm Turn (Alemana Turn)*

Commence in Normal Hold. Precede with Basic Movement.

	Man	**Woman**	**Timing**
	Facing wall, weight on RF:	Backing wall, weight on LF:	
1	LF forward	RF back	2
2	Replace weight to RF, commencing to raise left arm	LF forward	3
3	LF closes to RF, commencing to lead woman to turn to Right	RF forward, commencing to turn Right	4 1
4	RF back, leading woman to turn to Right under left arm, releasing hold with right hand	LF forward, turning Right under right arm, releasing left hand	2
5	Replace weight to LF, continuing to turn partner under left arm	RF forward, still turning under right arm	3
6	RF closes to LF, lowering left arm and taking normal hold	LF forward, having completed one turn to Right over Steps 3–6, lowering right arm and taking Normal Hold	4 1

Note: When followed by Hand-to-Hand, Step 6 will be to side, taking Double Hold.

Follow with Basic Movement or Hand-to-Hand.

10 Hand to Hand

Commence in Double Hold, feet apart. Precede with Woman's Under Arm Turn (Alemana Turn).

	Man Facing wall. Weight on RF:	**Woman** Backing wall. Weight on LF:	**Timing**
1	LF back in Right Side-by-Side Position, turning ¼ turn to Left, releasing hold with left hand	RF back, turning ¼ to Right, releasing hold with right hand	2
2	Replace weight to RF	Replace weight to LF	3
3	LF to side, turning ¼ to Right, taking woman's right hand in left hand	RF to side, turning ¼ to Left	4 1
4	RF back in Left Side-by-side position, turning ¼ to Right, releasing hold with right hand	LF back, turning ¼ to Left, releasing hold with left hand	2
5	Replace weight to LF	Replace weight to RF	3
6	RF to side, turning ¼ to Left	LF to side, turning ¼ to Right	4 1
	Finish facing wall	Finish backing wall	

Note: From the time that the man takes Double Hold at the end of the preceding step, both arms should be kept steady.

Steps 1–6 may be repeated. Follow with Basic Movement or Alternative Basic Movement.

11 Alternative Basic Movement

Commence in Normal Hold, feet apart. Precede with Hand to Hand or
New York.

	Man Facing wall, or LOD, weight on RF:	**Woman** Backing wall, or LOD, weight on LF:	**Timing**
1	Close LF to RF	Close RF to LF	2
2	Replace weight on RF	Replace weight on LF	3
3	LF to side	RF to side	4 1
4	Close RF to LF	Close LF to RF	2
5	Replace weight to LF	Replace weight to RF	3
6	RF to side	LF to side	4 1

Follow with Basic Movement.

12 Spot (or Solo) Turn to Left or Right

	Man (or Woman) Turn to Right:	**Woman (or Man)** Turn to Left:	**Timing**
1	LF fwd commencing to turn Right	RF fwd commencing to turn Left	2
2	RF fwd continue to turn Right	LF fwd continue to turn Left	3
3	LF to side to complete turn, to end facing partner (having made one complete turn almost on the spot)	RF to side to complete turn to Left, to end facing partner (having made one complete turn almost on the spot)	4, 1

Note: These are danced solo either to Left or Right. Release hold at
end of previous figure.

Choreography

(a)   Basic Movement.
         Shoulder to Shoulder.
         Side Step (Turning).
         Cucaracha to Left.
         Cucaracha to Right.

(b)   First half Basic Movement.
         Six Backward Progressive Walks.
         Natural Top.
         First half Basic Movement.
         Side Rock.
         New York.

(c)   Woman's Under Arm Turn (Alemana Turn).
         Hand to Hand; Alternative Basic Movement.
         Basic Movement.

(d)   Basic Movement.
         New York.
         Alternative Basic Movement.
         Basic Movement.

(e)   First half of Basic Movement.
         Natural Top.
         Side Step.
         Basic Movement.

(f)   Basic Movement.
         Side Step.
         Cucaracha to Left.
         Cucaracha to Right.
         Basic Movement.

(g)   Basic Movement.
         New York.
         Side Step (Turning).

8

—————— SAMBA ——————

The Samba is an animated dance with a strong and characteristic rhythm. It originated in Africa and was taken to Bahia in the north of Brasil by the slaves sent to work on the sugar plantations. The dance gradually lost its ritualistic nature and eventually became the Brasilian national dance.

It was carnival time in Rio de Janeiro that first put the Samba on the Western map. The Bahians and others from the sugar plantations and villages travelled to Rio for the yearly festivities. Gradually the subtle beat and interpretative nuances of the Samba began to take over in the street dancing, the cafés and the ballrooms until, eventually it became the musical and dancing soul of Brasil.

Originally, the dance had very characteristic hand movements, derived from its ritualistic function, when small containers of aromatic herbs were held in each hand and moved in front of the nose to 'drug' the dancer with the exciting fragrance. There was much solo work and, before it became a ballroom dance, it contained steps incorporated from the Indian *Maxixe* (pronounced as *Mah-chee-chay*).

The great American dancers, Irene and Vernon Castle, used the Samba in their professional routines, and so it began to spread. But it was probably Carmen Miranda, the best known Brasilian of them all, who, with her tremendous vitality and showmanship, gave the Samba its established place as one of the most exciting and catching rhythms in the world. In Brasil the *Samba Schools* grew and flourished and the country has now developed its own balletic art which has the Samba rhythm and basic movements as a marked contribution.   (G.W.)

───────────────── **The dance** ─────────────────

Music and hold

This is written in 2/4 time, 2 beats to a bar of music, counted *One, two*. In the Side, Natural and Reverse Basic Movements one beat is given to each step. In the Side, Natural and Reverse Alternative Basic Movements, counted *One a two* ('*a*' denotes the quarter beat), ¾ of a beat is given to the first step, ¼ of a beat to the second step and one beat to the third step. The hold is similar to the Rumba. Tempo of music should be 50 BPM (beats per minute).

Footwork

All steps are taken Ball Flat except the quarter beat steps which are taken on the ball of the foot only. The term *part weight* denotes that weight is taken only momentarily on the foot as the next step is taken.

Knee action

The Basic Bounce and Alternative Basic Bounce, so typical of the Samba, come from the flexing and straightening of the knees, with a slight elevation at the end of each beat of music.

In the basic bounce, with two steps to a bar of music, counted *One, two*, the knees are flexed when weight is taken on the stepping foot, and the straightening takes place between each step.

In the Alternative Basic Bounce, three steps to a bar of music, counted *One a two*, the knees are flexed when weight is taken on the stepping foot, first step, straightened on the second step, flexed on the third step, straightening between this and the following step.

Figures

As several of the figures in the Samba are progressive it is preferable to take these moving around the room. Suggested alignments are given with all figures.

1 Rhythm Bounce

Commence in Normal Hold. Precede with Whisk to Right.

	Man Facing wall, weight on RF:	**Woman** Backing wall, weight on LF:	**Timing**
1	LF to side and slightly back, right knee bent and veering towards left knee	RF to side and slightly back, left knee bent and veering towards right knee	1
2–7	Keep feet in place and with a slight bounce action, swing hips slightly to – RLRLRL	Just as for man but LRLRLR	a 2 a 1 a 2

Follow with Whisk to Right or Volta to Right.

2 Side Basic Movement

(a) With Basic Bounce

Commence in Normal Hold.

	Man Facing wall, weight on RF:	**Woman** Back wall, weight on LF:	**Timing**
1	LF to side	RF to side	1
2	RF closes to LF, with pressure, without weight	LF closes to RF, with pressure, without weight	2
3	RF to side	LF to side	1
4	LF closes to RF, with pressure, without weight	RF closes to LF, with pressure without weight	2

(b) With Alternative Basic Bounce

Commence in Normal Hold.

	Man Facing wall, weight on RF:	**Woman** Backing wall, weight on LF:	**Timing**
1	LF to side	RF to side	1
2	RF closes to LF	LF closes to RF	a
3	Replace weight to LF	Replace weight to RF	2
4	RF to side	LF to side	1
5	LF closes to RF	RF closes to LF	a
6	Replace weight to RF	Replace weight to LF	2

3 Basic Movement Forward and Backward

(a) Turning to Right

Commence in Normal Hold, using Basic Bounce.

	Man Facing LOD, weight on LF:	**Woman** Backing LOD, weight on RF:	**Timing**
1	RF forward	LF back	1
2	LF closes to RF with pressure, without weight	RF closes to LF, with pressure, without weight	2
3	LF back	RF forward	1
4	RF closes to LF, with pressure, without weight	LF closes to RF, with pressure without weight	2

A gradual turn to the Right is made throughout. May also be danced without turn.

(b) Alternative Basic Movement Forward and Backward

Commence in Normal Hold, using Alternative Basic Bounce.

	Man Facing LOD, weight on LF:	**Woman** Backing LOD, weight on RF:	**Timing**
1	RF forward	LF back	1
2	LF closes to RF	RF closes to LF	a
3	Replace weight to RF	Replace weight to LF	2
4	LF back	RF forward	1
5	RF closes to LF	LF closes to RF	a
6	Replace weight to LF	Replace weight to RF	2

Note: Basic Movements may be danced in any alignment.

A gradual turn to the Right is made throughout. May also be danced without turn.

(c) Basic Movement Forward and Backward Turning to Left

Commence in Normal Hold, using Basic Bounce.

	Man Facing LOD, weight on RF:	**Woman** Backing LOD, weight on LF:	**Timing**
1	LF forward	RF back	1
2	RF closes to LF, with pressure without weight	LF closes to RF, with pressure, without weight	2
3	RF back	LF forward	1
4	LF closes to RF, with pressure without weight	RF closes to LF, with pressure, without weight	2

A gradual turn to the Left is made throughout. May also be danced without turn.

(d) Alternative Basic Movement Forward and Backward Turning to Left

Commence in Normal Hold, using Alternative Basic Bounce.

	Man Facing LOD, weight on RF:	**Woman** Backing LOD, weight on LF:	**Timing**
1	LF forward	RF back	1
2	RF closes to LF	LF closes to RF	a
3	Replace weight to LF	Replace weight to RF	2
4	RF back	LF forward	1
5	LF closes to RF	RF closes to LF	a
6	Replace weight to RF	Replace weight to LF	2

Note: Reverse Basic Movements may be danced in any alignment.

A gradual turn to the Left is made throughout. May also be danced without turn.

4 *Whisks*

(a) Whisk to Right

Commence in Normal Hold, using Alternative Basic Bounce. Precede with Right Basic Movement or Whisk to Left.

	Man Facing wall, weight on LF:	**Woman** Backing wall, weight on RF:	**Timing**
1	RF to side	LF to side	1
2	LF behind RF, toe to heel, toe slightly turned out	RF behind LF, toe to heel, toe slightly turned out	a
3	Replace weight to RF	Replace weight to LF	2

Follow with Left (Reverse) Basic Movement, Rhythm Bounce, Whisk to Left, or Samba Walks, turning to Promenade Position to face LOD on the Whisk.

(b) Whisk to Left

Commence in Normal Hold, using Alternative Basic Bounce. Precede with Left Basic Movement, Whisk to Right, Samba Walks in Promenade Position (see page 76), turning to face wall on the Whisk.

	Man Facing wall, weight on RF:	**Woman** Backing wall, weight on LF:	**Timing**
1	LF to side	RF to side	1
2	RF behind LF, toe to heel, toe slightly turned out	LF behind RF, toe to heel, toe slightly turned out	a
3	Replace weight to LF	Replace with RF	2

5   Samba Walks in Promenade Position

Commence in Promenade Position, with feet pointing to LOD. Use very slight Alternative Basic Bounce. Precede with Whisk to Right, or Side Basic Movement turning to Promenade Position.

	Man Facing LOD, weight on RF:	**Woman** Facing LOD, weight on LF:	**Timing**
1	LF forward	RF forward	1
2	RF back, small step, part weight	LF back, small step, part weight	a
3	Draw LF slightly towards RF	Draw RF slightly towards LF	2
4	RF forward	LF forward	1
5	LF back, small step, part weight	RF back, small step, part weight	a
6	Draw RF slightly towards LF	Draw LF slightly towards RF	2

Steps 1–6 may be repeated. End in Promenade Position. Follow with Side Basic Movement or Whisk to Left, turning to face partner.

1–3 are the LF Samba Walk, 4–6 are the RF Samba Walk.

6   Volta Movements

(a)   Volta Turning to Left

Commence in Normal Hold, slightly apart, using Alternative Basic Bounce. Precede with Volta to Right or Whisk to Right.

Man Facing wall, weight on RF:	**Woman** Backing wall, weight on LF:	**Timing**

	Man	Woman	Timing
1	LF in front of RF, heel to toe, left toe turned out	RF in front of LF, heel to toe, right toe turned out	1
2	RF to side and slightly back, toe turned out	LF to side and slightly back, toe turned out	a
3	Draw LF in front of RF, heel to toe, left toe turned out	Draw RF in front of LF, heel to toe, right toe turned out	2
4–7	Repeat Steps 2 and 3 twice.	Repeat Steps 2 and 3 twice	a 1 a 2

A gradual turn, up to ¼, is made throughout. May also be danced without turn. Follow with Whisk to Right or Volta to Right.

(b) Volta Turning to Right

Commence in Normal Hold, slightly apart, using Alternative Basic Bounce. Precede with Rhythm Bounce or Volta to Left.

	Man	Woman	Timing
	Facing wall, weight on LF:	Backing wall, weight on RF:	
1	RF in front of LF, heel to toe, right toe turned out	LF in front of RF, heel to toe, left toe turned out	1
2	LF to side and slightly back, toe turned out	RF to side and slightly back, toe turned out	a
3	Draw RF in front of LF, heel to toe, right toe turned out	Draw LF in front of RF, heel to toe, left toe turned out	2
4–7	Repeat Steps 2 and 3 twice	Repeat Steps 2 and 3 twice	a 1 a 2

A gradual turn, up to ¼, is made throughout. May also be danced without turn. Follow with Whisk to Left or Volta to Left.

(c) Spot Volta to Right

Commence in Normal Hold, using Alternative Basic Bounce. Precede with Left Basic Movement or Whisk to Right.

	Man	**Woman**	**Timing**
	Facing wall or LOD, weight on RF:	Backing wall or LOD, weight on LF:	
1	Whisk to Left – LRL, raising left arm, releasing hold with –	RF in front of LF, heel to toe, right toe turned out, turning under right arm to right, releasing left hand	1
2	Right hand, and turning woman a complete –	LF to side and slightly back, still turning	a
3	Turn under arm to right	RF in front of LF, heel to toe, having completed a full turn to right	2
		The ball of the RF remains on one spot	

Finish in Normal Hold. Follow with Whisk to Right or Right (Natural) Basic Movement.

(d) Spot Volta to Left

Commence in Normal Hold, using Alternative Basic Bounce. Precede with Right Basic Movement or Whisk to Left.

	Man	**Woman**	**Timing**
	Facing wall or LOD, weight on LF:	Backing wall or LOD, weight on RF:	
1	Whisk to Right – RLR, raising left arm, releasing hold with –	LF in front of RF, heel to toe, left toe turned out, turning under right arm to left, releasing left hand	1
2	Right hand, and turning woman a complete –	RF to side and slightly back, still turning	a

	Man	Woman	Timing
3	Turn under arm to left	LF in front of RF, heel to toe, having completed a full turn to left	2
		The ball of the LF remains on one spot	

Finish in Normal Hold. Follow with Whisk to Left or Left Basic Movement.

7 Left Turn

Commence in Normal Hold, using Alternative Basic Bounce. Precede with Left Basic Movement.

	Man	Woman	Timing
	Facing LOD or diagonally centre:	Backing LOD or diagonally centre:	
1	LF forward, commencing to turn to left	RF back commencing to turn to left	1
2	RF to side and slightly back, continuing to turn to left	Left heel close to right heel continuing to turn to left	a
3	LF crosses in front of RF, toe turned out, continuing to turn to left	RF closes to LF continuing to turn to left	2
4	RF back and slightly rightwards, continuing to turn to left	LF forward continuing to turn to left	1
5	Left heel close to right heel, continuing to turn to left	RF to side and slightly back continuing to turn to left	a
6	RF closes to LF, continuing to turn to left	LF crosses in front of RF, toe turned out continuing to turn to left	2

7/8 turn or less is made over Steps 1–6. Follow with Left Basic Movement.

——————— Choreography ———————

(a) Rhythm Bounce.
   Side Basic Movement.
   Whisk to Right and to Left.
   Promenade Walks.
   Whisk to Left and to Right.
   Right (Natural) Basic.

(b) Reverse Basic Movement.
   Side Basic Movement, turning to face LOD.
   Four Samba Walks in Promenade Position.
   Side Basic Movement, turning to face wall.

(c) Whisks to Left and Right.
   Rhythm Bounce.
   Volta to Right.
   Volta to Left.
   Natural Basic Movement.

(d) Reverse Turn, to face wall.
   Whisks to Left and Right.
   Two Stationary Samba Walks.
   Spot Volta to Right.
   Whisk to Right.
   Reverse Basic Movement.

9

———— **CHA CHA CHA** ————

The Cha Cha Cha is perhaps the most popular of the Latin dances. The name rolls off the tongue, and the rhythm is easy to understand. The dance almost speaks for itself through the music where the beat of the Bongo Drums and the Marracas seem to say *Cha, Cha Cha, Step, Step.*

The dance originally came from Cuba and its forerunner is the Mambo, which is fast and more for the specialist. This developed into the Triple Mambo (hence the three counts) but gradually a slower, more pronounced and clearer interpretation of the rhythm was evolved, called the Cha Cha Cha (sometimes referred to as the Cha Cha). Music arrangers seemed able to adapt many popular melodies to the Cha Cha Cha rhythm, thus creating continuous interest in the dance.   (P.S.)

———————— **The dance** ————————

Music

Take care to buy records that are written as Cha Cha Chas, and if possible begin with a slow one. When a dancer is efficient he can begin the dance with the Cha Cha Cha Chasse, or with the forward step on the left foot. Some dancers even prefer to commence with the backward half of the Basic Movement. There is no set rule about this. Because of its Latin parentage the rhythm is felt in the hips more than in the feet, although of course it is essential to learn the foot positions first. It is not necessary to have a large repertoire of figures because the feeling of the music is satisfaction in itself. Five or six figures would be more than enough, and with practice these can be changed around to make interesting and challenging patterns, always remembering, of course, the art of leading or following your partner into the change of figures. Tempo: 30 to 34 bars to the minute.

Footwork and hold

As in the Jive and Rock, the man plays a leading and supporting role and in many advanced figures the girl has the more active part of the dance, turning under arm and moving away from and towards her partner. The steps should be small and rhythmic with the emphasis on the hips and body rhythm as in all Latin dances. Rhythm is the essence of the dance. The hold is similar to the Rumba and Samba, just slightly apart from partner, and some figures are danced without hold, such as the Time Steps. The footwork is ball flat throughout, and when stepping backwards the heel will lower later than when stepping forward, in order to avoid the weight dropping backwards. Good poise, balance and strong positive leg and foot action are essential to achieve the feeling of the Cha Cha Cha.

How to learn the dance

First work on the Cha Cha Cha Chasses to right and to left. Mark out the three steps keeping each step small, and give slightly more time to the third step; feel quite a positive pause, in fact to count *Cha Cha pause* is a very good way to rehearse. When the feeling of the two Chasses has been achieved, then practise the two steps that link the Chasses together, making sure that each step is a positive foot and weight change, like marking time. Then put the first five steps into one unit, first making sure that you have five positive steps in the first half, and five positive steps in the second half. Having achieved this continue to *practise* the ten steps that make the basic pattern, because this Basic Movement is the foundation upon which all the other step patterns are built.

Figures

1 RF and LF Cha Cha Cha Chasse

Right foot Cha Cha Cha Chasse: commence feet apart.

	Man	**Woman**	**Timing**
1	Small step to side RF	Small step to side LF	4
2	Move LF slightly towards RF	Move RF slightly towards LF	&
3	Very small step to side RF	Very small step to side LF	1

Left foot Cha Cha Cha Chasse: Commence feet apart.

1	Small step to side LF	Small step to side RF	4
2	Move RF slightly towards LF	Move LF slightly towards RF	&
3	Very small step to side LF	Very small step to side RF	1

2 Basic Movement in place

Commence feet apart. For practice face wall.

	Man	**Woman**	**Timing**
1	Step on LF in place	Step on RF in place	2
2	Step on RF in place	Step on LF in place	3
3–5	Dance a LF Chasse	Dance a RF Chasse	4&1
6	Step on RF in place	Step on LF in place	2

	Man	**Woman**	**Timing**
7	Step on LF in place	Step on RF in place	3
8–10	Dance a RF Chasse	Dance a LF Chasse	4&1

3 Basic Movement

Commence in normal hold, feet apart, weight on RF facing wall. Figure turns gradually left.

	Man	**Woman**	**Timing**
1	LF forward commencing to turn to L	RF back commencing to turn L	2
2	Replace weight to RF continuing to turn	Replace weight to LF continuing to turn	3
3–5	LF to side and slightly back to Chasse LRL continuing turning to L	RF to side to Chasse RLR, continuing turning to L	4&1
6	RF back continuing to turn L	LF forward continuing to turn L	2
7	Replace weight to LF continuing to turn	Replace weight to RF continuing to turn	3
8–10	RF to side to Chasse RLR continuing to turn L to face centre	LF to side and slightly back to Chasse LRL continuing to turn L to back centre	4&1

Note: The Basic Movement may be danced with or without turn to Left.

End in normal hold. Finish in direction required for next figure i.e. if New York is next figure, end facing wall.

4 New York

Commence in normal hold, feet apart, weight on RF, facing wall. Precede with the Basic Movement, releasing hold with R hand ready to step into L Side-by-Side Position.

	Man	**Woman**	**Timing**
1	Turning to R, LF forward in L Side-by-Side position, facing against LOD	Turning to L, RF forward in L Side-by-Side position, facing against LOD	2
2	Replace weight to RF commencing to turn to L	Replace weight to LF commencing to turn to R	3
3–5	LF to side to Chasse LRL turning L to face wall and woman, releasing hold with L hand and taking the woman's L hand in R hand	RF to side to Chasse RLR turning R to face centre and man	4&1
6	Turning to L, RF forward in R Side-by-Side position, facing LOD	LF forward in R Side-by-Side position, facing LOD	2
7	Replace weight to LF commencing to turn to R	Replace weight to RF commencing to turn to L	3
8–10	RF to side to Chasse RLR turning R to face wall and woman, releasing hold with R hand and taking woman's R hand in L hand	LF to side to Chasses LRL turning L to face centre and man	4&1

Follow with a Spot Turn (man turning R and woman L) or a Basic

Movement *or* repeat Steps 1–5 and follow with a Spot Turn (man turning L and woman R).

5 Time Step

Commence in Normal or Open Facing Position with or without hold, feet apart, weight on RF or LF and commencing direction according to choreography.

	Man	**Woman**	**Timing**
	LF Time Step:	RF Time Step:	
1	LF behind RF toe slightly turned out	RF behind LF	2
2	Replace weight to RF	Replace weight to LF	3
3–5	LF to side to Chasse LRL	RF to side to Chasse RLR	4&1
	RF Time Step:	LF Time Step:	
1	RF behind LF toe slightly turned out	LF behind RF	2
2	Replace weight to LF	Replace weight to RF	3
3–5	RF to side to Chasse RLR	LF to side to Chasse LRL	4&1

Note: For precedes and follows see **Choreography**.

6 Shoulder to Shoulder

Commence in normal hold (or without hold), weight on RF slightly forward. Precede with Spot Turn or Basic Movement preparing to step outside partner on her L side.

	Man	**Woman**	**Timing**
1	LF forward outside partner on L side	RF back	2
2	Replace weight to RF	Replace weight to LF	3

	Man	**Woman**	**Timing**
3–5	LF to side to Chasse LRL turning ¼ to L	RF to side to Chasse RLR turning ¼ to L	4&1
6	RF forward outside partner on R side	LF back	2
7	Replace weight to LF	Replace weight to RF	3
8–10	RF to side to Chasse RLR turning ¼ to R	LF to side to Chasse LRL turning ¼ to R	4&1

Repeat Steps 1–5 to end in Promenade Position and follow with a Spot Turn (man turning to L and woman to R) or Repeat Steps 1–10 to end in Closed Facing Position.

7   Side Basic

Commence facing partner with or without hold, weight on RF. Precede with Basic Movement or 1–5 of New York into Steps 6–10 of Side Basic.

	Man	**Woman**	**Timing**
1	LF to side	RF to side	2
2	RF closes to LF	LF closes to RF	3
3	LF to side	RF to side	4
4	RF closes towards LF	LF closes towards RF	&
5	LF to side	RF to side	1
6	RF closes to LF	LF closes to RF	2
7	LF to side	RF to side	3
8	RF closes towards LF	LF closes towards RF	4
9	LF to side	RF to side	&
10	RF closes to LF	LF closes to RF	1

8   Three Cha Cha Chas

These are three Cha Cha Cha Chasses danced forward, backward or forward side-by-side, counted 4 and 1, 2 and 3, 4 and 1.

In Right Side-by-Side Position: After 2 or 12 of Hand to Hand, 3 Forward Chasses for man and woman.

No turn, or turn slightly towards partner on the first and third Chasses and slightly away on the second Chasse.

Follow with Spot Turn to Left (woman to Right).

9   Spot Turn

These are usually danced individually, but may be danced together, in which case man dances a Left turn while woman dances a Right turn, or vice versa.

	Spot Turn to Right, Man or Woman	**Spot Turn to Left, Man or Woman**	**Timing**
1	LF forward turning to R making approx ⅜ turn to R	RF forward turning to L making approx ⅜ turn to L	2
2	RF forward continuing to turn approx ⅜	LF forward continuing to turn approx ⅜	3
3–5	Still turning approx ¼ to R Chasses sideways LRL Amount of Turn: 1 complete turn End facing partner	Still turning approx ¼ to L Chasse sideways RLR Amount of Turn: 1 complete turn End facing partner	4&1

10   Woman's Under Arm Turn to Right (Alemana Turn)

Commence in Normal Hold, feet apart. Precede with Basic Movement.

	Man	**Woman**	**Timing**
1	LF forward	RF back	2
2	Replace weight on to RF	Replace weight on to LF	3
3–5	Cha Cha Cha Chasse in place (LRL)	Cha Cha Cha Chasse (RLR) to side commencing to turn to R	4&1
6	RF back leading partner to turn to R under L arm releasing hold with R hand	LF forward still turning	2
7	Replace weight on LF	RF forward still turning	3
8–10	Cha Cha Cha Chasse to side. Regain normal hold	Still turning to R Cha Cha Cha Chasse (LRL) to side to end facing partner. Regain normal hold	4&1

Follow with Basic Movement or Hand to Hand.

11 Hand to Hand

Commence in Normal Facing Position in Double Hold, feet apart, man facing wall. Precede with the Woman's Under Arm Turn (Alemana Turn).

	Man	**Woman**	**Timing**
1	Turning to L, LF back in R Side-by-Side position, backing against LOD releasing hold with L hand	Turning ¼ to R, RF back in R Side-by-Side position releasing hold with R hand	2
2	Replace weight on RF commencing to turn to R	Replace weight on to LF commencing to turn L	3

	Man	Woman	Timing
3–5	LF to side to Chasse LRL turning R to face wall and woman and taking double hold	RF to side to Chasse RLR turning to L to face centre and partner	4&1
6	Turning to R and releasing hold with R hand, RF back in L Side-by-Side position, backing LOD	Turning ¼ to L, LF back in L Side-by-Side position	2
7	Replace weight on LF commencing to turn L	Replace weight on RF commencing to turn R	3
8–10	RF to side to Chasse RLR turning L to face wall and the woman taking double hold in Closed Facing Position	LF to side to Chasse LRL	4&1

Repeat Steps 1–10 or follow with Basic Movement.

Repeat Steps 1–5 and follow with a Spot Turn (man turning to L and woman to R).

12 Forward and Back Run

Commence in Normal Hold. Precede with the Basic Movement. This can be used by the woman and the man dancing normal opposite or is great fun when man moves back away from the woman and she moves back away from man and then both return and continue into New York or Basic Movement.

	Man	Woman	Timing
1	LF forward	RF back	2
2	Replace weight to RF	Replace weight to LF	3
3–5	Three small steps travelling back, passing feet, LRL	Three small steps travelling forward, passing feet, RLR	4&1

Note: Steps 1 and 2 are almost in place.

	Man	**Woman**	**Timing**
6	RF back	LF forward	2
7	Replace weight to LF	Replace weight to RF	3
8–10	Three small steps travelling forward, passing feet, RLR	Three small steps travelling back, passing feet, LRL	4&1

Note: Steps 1, 2, 6 and 7 are almost in place.

Choreography

(a) Basic Movement (repeated)
New York, then repeat 1–5
Spot Turn to L for Man
Spot Turn to R for Woman
   Continue into Basic Movement

(b) Basic Movement (repeated)
Woman's Under Arm Turn (Alemana Turn)
Two Time Steps
   Continue into Basic Movement

(c) Basic Movement
Alemana Turn
Hand to Hand. Repeat Steps 1–5
Spot Turn to L for Man
(Spot Turn to R for Woman)

(d) Basic Movement
New York
Side Basic
Back Run (Both travelling back)
Forward Run (Both travelling forward)
New York. Repeat 1–5
Spot Turn to L for Man
(Spot Turn to R for Woman)
   Continue into Basic Movement

(e)   Alemana Turn to end with Double Hand Hold
      Hand to Hand. Repeat Steps 1 and 2
      Three Cha Cha Chasses forward in R Side-by-Side Position
      Spot Turn to L for Man
      (Spot Turn to R for Woman)
         Continue with Basic Movement

10
———————— JIVE ————————

The Jive was brought to England from the United States by the GIs during the Second World War. It caused a great change in the English ballroom dancing scene. The atmosphere of 'live for today and let tomorrow look after itself' caused by the war set a pattern for dancing with a very carefree style. The dance developed on rather athletic lines and became 'Jitterbug', with lifts and exciting jumps. Because of this it was unsuitable and dangerous for the public ballroom and was banned except as a competition dance; it then went through many stages and became known by various names such as *Lindy, West Coast Swing, American Swing, Rock and Roll,* and probably more. Although each new title brought with it something slightly different, the same base was there: the man would turn the woman under his arm from left to right, sometimes spinning her, sometimes passing her behind his back, but mainly marking the rhythm and leading the lady to dance the shapes by turning and spinning.

The Jive was then groomed by dancing teachers and a dance emerged which could be taught and danced as a social or exhibition dance. The Rock and Roll was based on the same shapes but with an easier, less energetic timing. Both have a place and very often a good Jive dancer combines the two dances.

The Jive is a non-progressive dance and can be danced in a fairly small space when the floor is crowded.

This dance is a *must* for any social dancer because, with the revival of the Big Band sound, the music is played many times during an average dance.   (P.S.)

The dance

Hold

This is similar to other Latin dances but easier and more relaxed, with the arms held slightly lower. The man must learn to get music 'in his hands' to give the correct lead to the woman because most of the 'talking' is done with hands. The knees must have a slight, springy action, not a pronounced bounce, but must be very pliable to cope with the speed of the music.

Footwork

All steps are taken on the ball of the foot with the heel lightly lowering to the floor. Knees are naturally flexed. The individual steps are small.

Chasse

A group of three steps taken sideways to right or left, backwards or forwards, or turning to right or left. The chasse is counted *Three a four* and is usually danced in sets of two: *Three a four, three a four*. The feet do not close on the second step as this would make the steps rather too sharp.

It is advisable to practise the chasse to the left and to the right with the linking back step many, many times before attempting to put any of the other figures together.

Initial exercise

The following exercise will help the beginner to feel the dance rhythm in the feet and hands before embarking on the actual step patterns that will eventually become his or her Jive. There are no real alignments although some are given as a guide to the beginner.

Commence facing the wall, feet very slightly apart, weight on RF, hands held in front as though holding partner with both hands, keeping them slightly low and loose at the wrist. Dance three very small steps (Jive chasse) almost in place, travelling slightly to left and using hands to the same timing as though turning left in the car, left hand down. Now follow with three small steps almost in place, travelling slightly to right and turning hands to normal position. Step back with left foot, small step (woman RF) with slight pulling action from hands, replace weight into RF in place and return hands to original position, so the little dance would go something like this: 1 2 3 – 4 5 6 – back, step.

A very slight pause will be felt on Steps 3 and 6 with a positive change of weight on the 'back, step'. Try this exercise until the steps fit quite fast music and make sure to use the hands in time with the music.

This little exercise can then be turned to the left, making a ¼ turn each time; first sequence commences facing wall, second one facing Line of Dance, third one facing centre, fourth one facing against Line of Dance, fifth one facing wall, having returned to original position. This will help the man particularly to understand how the dance turns to the left, and the ¼ turn is the amount of turn he will normally make. The lady, of course, will turn more when she eventually turns under arm and so on.

When practising this turn to left, the value of the left hand down on the first chasse will be felt to help the body to get a slight sway to the left as though turning a corner in a car or on a bicycle. The man will make his steps very, very small as he is on the inside of the circle, the lady slightly larger because she has the outside of the circle to follow. The ability to dance this exercise well will make the study and dancing of the rest of the figures in the Jive reasonably easy.

Figures

1 Jive Chasses to Left and Right

(Man or Woman) Commence in Normal Hold or Double Hand Hold, man facing wall, knees softly flexed.

	Chasse to Left	**Chasse to Right**	**Timing**
1	LF to side (small step)	RF to side (small step)	3
2	Close RF towards LF	Close LF towards RF	a
3	LF to side (small step)	RF to side (small step)	4
	Chasse to Right	**Chasse to Left**	
4	RF to side (small step)	LF to side (small step)	3
5	Close LF towards RF	Close RF towards LF	a
6	RF to side (small step)	LF to side (small step)	4

2 Fallaway Rock

Commence in Normal Hold, weight on RF, facing wall. Precede with Chasse to Right (RLR).

	Man	**Woman**	**Timing**
1	LF back in Fallaway turning ⅛ to left turning the woman to R	RF back in Fallaway turning ⅛ to right	1
2	Replace weight forward to RF in Promenade Position commencing to turn the woman to L	Replace weight forward to LF in Promenade Position	2
3–5	LF to side to Chasse LRL turning R to face wall	RF to side to Chasse RLR turning L to face centre	3a4
6–8	RF to side to Chasse RLR	LF to side to Chasse LRL	3a4

End in Closed Facing Position. Follow with Change of Places Right to Left or Fallaway Throwaway.

3 Fallaway Throwaway

Commence in normal hold, weight on RF, facing wall.

	Man	**Woman**	**Timing**
1–5	1–5 of Fallaway Rock (LRLRL). On Step 5 lower joined hands and lean slightly to L	1–5 of Fallaway Rock (RLRLR). Lean slightly to R on Step 5	1 2 3a4
6–8	RF forward to Chasse RLR turning L to face LOD, leading the woman to move away and releasing hold with R hand	LF back to Chasse LRL turning L to back LOD	3a4

End in Open Facing Position. Follow with Link Rock *or* Change of Places Left to Right.

4 Link Rock

Commence in Open Facing Position, weight on RF, direction according to preceding figure.

	Man	**Woman**	**Timing**
1	LF back	RF back	1
2	Replace weight forward to RF	Replace weight forward to LF	2
3–5	LF forward to Chasse LRL leading the woman forward	RF forward to Chasse RLR	3a4
6–8	RF to side to Chasse RLR regaining normal hold	LF to side Chasse LRL regaining normal hold	3a4

End in Closed Facing Position. Follow with Fallaway Rock.

5   Link and Whip

Commence in Open Facing Position, weight on RF. Direction according to preceding figure.

	Man	**Woman**	**Timing**
1	LF back	RF back	1
2	Replace weight forward to RF	Replace weight forward to LF	2
3–5	LF forward to Chasse LRL to end LF diagonally forward, having led the woman forward, regaining normal hold	RF forward to Chasse RLR to end with RF forward between partner's feet, regaining normal hold	3a4
6	RF crosses behind LF commencing to turn R	LF forward towards Man's R side, turning R	1
7	LF to side (small step) continuing to turn R	RF forward between partner's feet, small step	2
8–10	R to side, very small step, to Chasse RLR completing required amount of turn to end in Fallaway position	LF to side to Chasse LRL continuing to turn R, ending in Fallaway position	3a4

End in Fallaway position. Follow with Change of Places R to L *or* Walks in Promenade Position.

Note: Up to a complete turn can be made.

6 Change of Places Right to Left

Commence in Normal Hold, weight on RF, facing wall.

	Man	**Woman**	**Timing**
1–5	1–5 of Fallaway Rock LRLRL. On Step 5 raise joined hands and commence to turn the woman to her R	1–5 of Fallaway Rock RLRLR. On Step 5 commence to turn to R	1 2 3a4
6–8	RF forward to Chasse RLR turning L to face LOD leading woman to complete her turn to R under the raised arms, having released hold with R hand. Lower joined hands at end of the woman's turn	Continue to turn to R under the raised arms and Chasse LRL to end LF back, backing LOD	3a4

End in Open Position. Follow with the Change of Places from Left to Right or Link Rock.

7 Change of Places Left to Right

Commence in Open Facing Position, weight on RF, facing LOD having danced Change of Places Right to Left.

	Man	**Woman**	**Timing**
1–2	1–2 of Link (LR)	1–2 of Link (RL)	1 2
3–5	Almost close LF to RF to Chasse LRL turning to R to face wall and leading the woman to turn to her L under the raised arms	Chasse RLR turning to L under the raised arms	3a4

	Man	**Woman**	**Timing**
6–8	RF forward to Chasse RLR leading woman to complete her turn to L and lowering the joined hands at end of the woman's turn	Continuing to turn L, LF back to Chasse LRL to end backing wall	3a4

End in Open Facing Position. Follow with Link Rock.

8 Change of Hands Behind Back

Commence in Open Facing Position, man facing wall, having danced Change of Places Left to Right.

	Man	**Woman**	**Timing**
1–2	1–2 of Link (LR)	1–2 of Link (RL)	1 2
3–5	Placing R hand over woman's R hand and releasing hold with L hand, LF forward to Chasse LRL leading woman forward to R side	RF forward to Chasse RLR moving to man's R side and commencing to turn to R	3a4
6–8	Changing woman's R hand into man's L behind his back, Chasse turning to L to face centre, RLR to end RF back	Chasse turning to R to face wall LRL to end LF back	3a4

Note: The man may place woman's R hand on his waist on Step 3, releasing hold with R hand and allowing the woman's R hand to trail around his waist, then catching it in his L hand again at the completion of his turn.

End in Open Facing Position. Follow with Link Rock.

9 Left Shoulder 'Shove'

Commence in L Side-by-Side Position, having danced Fallaway Throw-away, turning to end with partner on L side, facing wall.

	Man	**Woman**	**Timing**
1	LF back	RF back	1
2	Replace weight forward to RF	Replace weight to LF	2
3–5	LF to side to Chasse LRL. Move towards each other with shoulders touching	RF to side to Chasse RLR. Move towards each other with shoulders touching	3a4
6–8	Giving woman a slight push with L shoulder, RF to side to Chasse RLR. Move slightly away from each other	LF to side to Chasse LRL. Move slightly away from each other	3a4

End in Left Side-by-Side Position facing wall and continue into Link Rock turning to face partner on first step.

10 Walks in Promenade

Commence in Normal Hold, man facing wall.

	Man	**Woman**	**Timing**
1–2	1–2 of Fallaway Rock (LR)	1–2 of Fallaway Rock (RL)	1 2
3–5	LF diag. forward to Chasse LRL turning the woman to L	RF to side to Chasse RLR turning to L	3a4
6–8	RF forward and across in Promenade Position to Chasse RLR turning the woman to R	LF forward in Promenade Position to Chasse LRL turning to R	3a4

Steps 3–8 may be repeated. End in Promenade Position – continue into Steps 3 to 8 of Change of Places Right to Left.

An alternative method of dancing the Walks is to substitute single steps for the Chasses (i.e. LRLR QQQQ).

11 Kick Ball Change

Commence having danced Change of Places Right to Left. This action is used in place of 1–2 of the Link.

	Man	**Woman**	**Timing**
1	Flick LF forward	Flick RF forward	1
2	Place LF slightly back, approx toe of LF to heel of RF (Ball of foot)	Place RF slightly back, approx toe of RF to heel of LF (Ball of foot)	a
3	Replace weight on to RF in place	Replace weight on to LF in place	2

Note: This could be danced in Promenade Position to replace Steps 1, 2, Fallaway Rock.

———— Choreography ————

(a) Jive Chasses to L and R
   Fallaway Rock
   Fallaway Throwaway
   Link Rock

(b) Fallaway Rock
   Change of Places R to L
   Link Rock

(c) Fallaway Rock
   Change of Places R to L
   Change of Places L to R
   Link and Whip

(d)   Fallaway Throwaway to L Side-by-Side Position
Left Shoulder 'Shove'
Change of Hands behind Back
Link and Whip

(e)   Jive Chasses to Left and Right
Fallaway Rock
Walks in Promenade Position
Kick Ball Change in Promenade Position (LF Man)
(RF Woman). Repeat the Kick Ball Change
5–8 of Fallaway Throwaway
Link Rock

Note: The Jive Chasses to L and R are only used to start the dance.

11

—————— MAMBO ——————

This dance is part of the family of Cha Cha Cha and Cuban Rumba. Its step construction is almost identical to that of the Rumba, but the music is much faster and does occasionally change its musical emphasis. When first introduced into this country the music was much too fast for most dancers and the dance did not become popular. Even now the music is rather difficult for the average dancer. However, many people travelling to exotic countries near the Equator will find this music played and will wish to have a knowledge of the dance. The Mambo is enjoying a renewed popularity due to a number of films featuring the dance. (P.S.)

————————— The dance —————————

Music, footwork, hold and action

The music is a fast type of Rumba (36 bars a minute). The hold is a little higher and more compact than the Rumba and Cha Cha Cha because of the speed of this dance. The steps are kept small and very rhythmic, using many rock actions, almost as breathing time before the next set of steps. The action appears rather staccato, using speed to get into a figure and then the appearance of a slight pause when the figure is completed. The stance is very upright and almost regal.

Footwork is ball flat throughout, always remembering that the weight lowers late on the foot when taking a step back. The action is similar to the Rumba, but faster with less emphasis on hip action.

How to learn the dance

Practise first the six steps of the basic movement until the speed and rhythmic effect of the steps have been perfected, and then gradually add one of the extra figures, practising the basic and the new figure until this is comfortable. Continue like this until one of the suggested routines has been achieved. Do not try to have a long programme of steps, you will be more successful with just a few, danced well, which will need less 'thinking' time.

Commence facing the 'outside' wall with weight on RF and work all steps from and to this position – remembering that the dance turns to the left. The alignments given are only a guide to the beginner and need not be regularly adhered to when the dancer is proficient.

Figures

1 Basic

Commence in Closed Facing Position, man facing wall.

	Man	Woman	Timing
1	LF forward, commencing to turn to L	RF back, commencing to turn to L	2
2	Replace weight to RF, continuing to turn to L	Replace weight to LF, continuing to turn to L	3

	Man	**Woman**	**Timing**
3	LF to side and slightly back continuing to turn to back wall	RF to side, continuing to turn to face wall	4 1
4	RF back, continuing to turn to L	LF forward, continuing to turn to L	2
5	Replace weight to LF, continuing to turn to L	Replace weight to RF, continuing to turn to L	3
6	RF to side continuing to turn to face wall	LF to side and slightly back, continuing to turn to back wall	4 1

Less turn could be made.

2 Closed Fan

Commence in Closed Facing Position, man facing wall having danced Basic Movement.

	Man	**Woman**	**Timing**
1–3	3 steps of Basic Movement to end in Promenade Position	3 steps of Basic Movement to end in Promenade Position	2 3 4 1
4	RF back leading the partner forward outside on man's L side, turning strongly to L	LF forward outside partner on his L side	2
5	Replace weight to LF continuing to turn	RF back and to side turning to L	3
6	RF to side continuing to turn to face centre	LF to side continuing to turn to back centre	4 1

End in Closed Facing Position. This figure may be repeated.

3   New York Break and Open Rock

Commence in Closed Facing Position, man facing wall, having danced Closed Fan.

	Man	**Woman**	**Timing**
1	LF forward, small step turning to R to Counter Promenade Position	RF forward, small step, turning to L to Counter Promenade Position	2
2	Replace weight to RF commencing to turn L	Replace weight to LF commencing to turn to R	3
3	LF to side turning L to face the woman and wall	RF to side turning R to face man and centre	4 1
4	Rock to RF in place	Rock to LF in place	2
5	Rock to LF in place	Rock to RF in place	3
6	Rock to RF in place. Type of Cucaracha with feet apart	Rock to LF with place. Type of Cucaracha with feet apart	4 1

Repeat New York Break and Open Rock. Steps 4–6 (the Open Rock) may be danced after the Fallaway Break.

4   Shoulder to Shoulder and Alternative Basic Movement

Left shoulders

Commence in Closed Facing Position, facing diagonally to wall against LOD, weight on RF, having turned slightly to R on preceding Basic Movement ready to step outside partner on her L side.

	Man	**Woman**	**Timing**
1	LF forward outside partner on L side	Back RF	2

	Man	Woman	Timing
2	Replace weight to RF commencing to turn L	Replace weight to LF commencing to turn L	3
3	LF to side turning L to face partner and wall	RF to side turning L to face man and centre	4 1
4	Close RF to LF	Close LF to RF	2
5	Replace weight to LF	Replace weight to RF	3
6	Side RF preparing to step outside partner on her L side if repeating the figure	Side LF	4 1

End facing partner and wall if continuing into Basic Movement or diagonally to wall against LOD if repeating the figure.

Right shoulders

Commence in Closed Facing Position, man facing diagonally to wall, having danced 1–3 of Basic Movement turning slightly to L ready to step outside partner on her R side.

	Man	Woman	Timing
1	RF forward outside partner on R side, facing diagonally to wall	LF back	2
2	Replace weight to LF commencing to turn to R	Replace weight to RF commencing to turn to R	3
3	RF to side turning R to face partner and wall	LF to side turning R to face man and centre	4 1
4	Close LF to RF	Close RF to LF	2
5	Replace weight to RF	Replace weight to LF	3

Man	Woman	Timing
6 Side LF preparing to step outside partner on her L side if repeating the R Shoulder to Shoulder or finish facing wall if continuing into Basic Movement	Side RF	
		4 1

5 Cucaracha Movements

Commence in Closed Facing Position, man facing wall, having danced a Basic Movement, or with weight on LF, having danced 1–3 of Basic Movement or Fallaway Break.

Man	Woman	Timing
1 LF to side with part weight	RF to side	2
2 Replace weight to RF	Replace weight to LF	3
3 Close LF to RF	Close RF to LF	4 1

This movement may be danced commencing with either foot. Step 1 may be taken forward, diagonally forward, side, back or diagonally back.

6 Fallaway Break

Commence in Closed Facing Position, weight on RF, facing wall, having danced a Basic Movement.

Man	Woman	Timing
1 LF back in Fallaway	RF back in Fallaway	2
2 Replace weight to RF	Replace weight to LF	3

	Man		**Woman**		**Timing**
3	Close LF	turning R to	Close RF	turning L to	
	to RF	face woman	to LF	face man	
	or	and wall	or	and centre	
	LF to		RF to		
	side		side		4 1

Follow with Cucarachas or Open Rock.

Choreography

(a) Basic Movement – repeated
Closed Fan repeated
and ended in Counter Promenade Position if following with:
New York and Open Rock repeated
Continue into Basic Movement

(b) New York Break and Open Rock repeated
Basic Movement repeated
Left Shoulder to Shoulder and
Alternative Basic repeated

(c) Closed Fan repeated
Fallaway Break closing on Step 3
Cucaracha Movements to R, to L and to R
Repeat Fallaway Break stepping to side on third step
Open Rock
Continue into Basic Movement

12

—— BOSSA NOVA ——

The Bossa Nova is sometimes referred to as a jazzy Samba and the change in interpretation of the music brought about the dance. It has taken a long time to become popular, perhaps because the rhythm sounds rather 'busy' to the dancer and a little difficult to understand.   (P.S.)

—————— The dance ——————

Music

Use authentic Bossa Nova music or follow the current trend in the dance, which is to use Baion music – a type of slow Samba.

Many chart records have a strong Bossa Nova or Baion beat and the steps described fit the feeling of this music, which has a strong *Slow Quick Quick* rhythm.

Footwork, hold and action

Hold is as for the Rumba. The dance is felt in the hips whereas the Samba is felt in the knees. Thus, use a strong hip action, similar to the Rumba, not a knee bounce. Steps must be kept small.

Figures

The figures listed form an ideal routine, and the dancer will find it a most satisfying dance.

1 Side Basic

Commence in normal Latin hold, or dance without hold.

	Man	**Woman**	**Timing**
1	Side LF dragging RF slightly towards LF	Side RF dragging LF slightly towards RF	S
2	Close RF to LF	Close LF to RF	Q
3	Replace weight on LF	Replace weight on RF	Q
	Repeat commencing with other foot		SQQ
	Repeat for the total of four bars.		SQQ SQQ

2 Forward and Back Basic

	Man	**Woman**	**Timing**
1	Forward LF leaving RF in place	Back RF	S
2	Close RF to LF	Close LF to RF	Q
3	Replace weight on LF	Replace weight on RF	Q
4	Back RF leaving LF in place	Forward LF	S
	Close LF to RF	Close RF to LF	Q
6	Replace weight on RF in place	Replace weight on LF in place	Q
	Repeat for the total of four bars.		SQQ SQQ

3 *Cross Basic*

Man	Woman	Timing
1 Side LF leaving RF in place	Side RF	S
2 Cross RF behind LF	Cross LF behind RF	Q
3 Replace weight on LF	Replace weight on RF	Q
4 Side RF leaving LF in place	Side LF	S
5 Cross LF behind RF	Cross RF behind LF	Q
6 Replace weight on RF	Replace weight on LF	Q
Repeat for the total of four bars.		SQQ SQQ

4 *Solo Turn – Side Basic*

Man	Woman	Timing
1 LF to side in Promenade Position commencing to turn to L	RF to side in Promenade Position commencing to turn to R	S
2 Forward RF in Promenade Position continuing to turn to L	Forward LF, turning R	Q
3 Replace weight forward to LF continuing to turn to L	Weight forward to RF, turning R	Q
4 Side RF, still turning L	Side LF, still turning R	S
5 Close LF to RF, facing partner	Close RF to LF, facing partner	Q
6 Mark time on RF in place to end facing partner	Mark time on LF	Q
Repeat for the total of four bars.		SQQ SQQ

5 *Push Away*

	Man	**Woman**	**Timing**
1	LF back leaving RF in place at the same time 'pushing' the woman away with L hand. Release hold with R hand	RF back	S
2	Close RF to LF	Close LF to RF	Q
3	Replace weight to LF	Replace weight to RF	Q
4	RF forward leaving LF in place	LF forward	S
5	Close LF to RF, regaining normal hold	Close RF to LF	Q
6	Replace weight to RF	Replace weight to LF	Q
	Repeat for the total of four bars.		SQQ SQQ

6 *Face to Face and Back to Back*

	Man	**Woman**	**Timing**
1	LF forward, turning to L and commencing to back partner, releasing hold	RF forward, turning to R	S
2	RF to side, small step, still turning L to almost back partner	LF to side, small step, still turning	Q
3	Close LF to RF, having completed ½ turn to L. Now backing partner	Close RF to LF, having completed ½ turn to R to back partner	Q
4	RF forward, turning to R and commencing to face partner	LF forward, turning to L	S

	Man	**Woman**	**Timing**
5	LF to side, small step, still turning R to almost face partner	RF to side, small step, still turning L	Q
6	Close RF to LF, having completed ½ turn to R. Now facing partner	Close LF to RF having completed ½ turn to face partner	Q

Regain normal hold.

Repeat for the total of four bars.   SQQ SQQ

—————— Choreography ——————

It is suggested that these Bossa Nova figures lead on naturally from one to the next.

13

──────── MERENGUE ────────

The Merengue is the national dance of the Dominican Republic, and also to some extent, of Haiti, the neighbour sharing the island. Not only is the Merengue used on every dancing occasion in the Dominican Republic, but it is very popular throughout the Caribbean and South America, and is one of the standard Latin-American dances in the USA.

There is much variety in Merengue music and most South American bands play it well. Tempos vary a great deal and the Dominicans enjoy a sharp quickening in pace towards the latter part of the dance. Normally the most favoured routine at all the clubs and restaurants that run a dance floor is a slow Bolero, breaking into a Merengue, which becomes akin to a bright, fast Jive in its closing stages. Ideally suited to the small, crowded club floors, it is a dance that is easy to learn, giving rhythmic pleasure in its movement. It seems to be gaining steadily in popularity.   (G.W.)

The dance

Music

This is written in 2/4 time; 2 beats to a bar of music, each step taking one beat. The timing in the Side Walk differs slightly and is given in the description of the figure. The tempo is 55–60 bars per minute.

Hold and footwork

The hold is similar as for the Rumba, though Merengue is sometimes danced in closer hold. The footwork is ball flat throughout.

How to learn the dance

All the figures may be preceded and followed by the Basic Side Step and may commence with the man facing the wall and the woman backing the wall.

The Basic Movement is typically Latin American in character, with a soft and attractive hip action that belongs to the music. Knees and hips are kept relaxed, with the shoulders steady.

The left foot is first placed to the side without weight, the knee being slightly bent, while the weight is carried on the straight right leg, with the hips pushed slightly to the right. The hips initiate the transference of weight to the left foot, moving over to the left as that leg straightens, and the right foot is brought almost to close with the left, without weight. The hips swing to the right again; weight is taken on the RF and the movement is repeated with the side step to the left.

Figures

1 Basic in place

Man	Woman	Timing
Weight on RF:	Weight on LF:	
1 Weight on LF in place. Transfer weight to RF in place. Continue this marking time action using strong ball of foot to the phrasing of the music	Weight on RF in place. Transfer weight to LF in place. Continue this marking time action using strong ball of foot to the phrasing of the music	2

2 Basic Side Step

Commence in Normal Hold.

	Man	Woman	Timing
	Weight on RF:	Weight on LF:	
1	LF to side, small step	RF to side, small step	2
2	RF closes, or almost closes, to LF	LF closes, or almost closes, to RF	2
3–8	Repeat 1 and 2 three times	Repeat 1 and 2 three times	1 2 1 2 1 2

May be danced with a gradual turn to the left, in a circular pattern or without turn.

3 Basic Walk

Commence in Normal Hold.

	Man	Woman	Timing
	Weight on RF:	Weight on LF:	
1	LF forward	RF back	1

	Man	**Woman**	**Timing**
2	RF almost closes to LF	LF almost closes to RF	2
3–8	Repeat 1 and 2 three times	Repeat 1 and 2 three times	1 2 1 2 1 2

May be danced with a gradual turn to the left.

4 Basic Side Step to Fallaway

Commence in Normal Hold.

	Man Weight on RF:	**Woman** Weight on LF:	**Timing**
1–4	Dance 4 steps of the Basic Side Step	Dance 4 steps of the Basic Side Step	1 2 1 2
5	LF back in Fallaway Position, turning ⅛ to left	RF back in Fallaway Position, turning ⅛ to right	1
6	Replace weight to RF in Promenade Position	Replace weight to LF in Promenade Position	2
7–8	Basic Side Step LR, turning ⅛ to right to face partner	Basic Side Step RL, turning ⅛ to left to face partner	1 2

5 Separation

Commence in Normal Hold. Precede with the Basic Side Step.

	Man Weight on RF:	**Woman** Weight on LF:	**Timing**
1–8	Man and woman place hands on partner's shoulders and take eight small steps backwards, away from each other, hands moving down partner's arms to take a double hold		1 2 1 2
	Man – LRLRLRLR	**Woman** – RLRLRLRL	1 2 1 2

Man	Woman	Timing
9–16	Man and woman take eight small steps forward, reversing the hands movement, to take normal hold	1 2 1 2
Man – LRLRLRLR	**Woman** – RLRLRLRL	1 2 1 2

Follow with Basic Side Step or Promenade Flick.

6   Separation with arm circle

Commence in Normal Hold.

Man Weight on RF:	Woman Weight on LF:	Timing
1–16	Dance the Separation. On Steps 9–12 slowly change hands to a palm-to-palm contact and on Steps 13–16 gradually raise the hands and begin to circle them outwards	1 2 1 2 1 2 1 2
17–24	Repeat Steps 1–4 and 13–16, circling hands outwards and down and then up again to Normal Hold	1 2 1 2 1 2 1 2

Follow with Basic Side Step or Promenade Flick.

7   Left and Right Turn

Commence in Normal Hold. Precede with Basic Side Step or Basic Side Step to Fallaway.

Man Weight on RF:	Woman Weight on LF:	Timing
1	LF forward, turning to left	RF back, turning to left	1
2	RF almost closes to LF, still turning	LF almost closes to RF, still turning	2

	Man	**Woman**	**Timing**
3–6	Repeat Steps 1 and 2 twice LRLR	Repeat Steps 1 and 2 twice RLRL	1 2 1 2
7	LF back, releasing right hand, pushing the woman slightly back	RF back, releasing left hand	1
8	Replace weight to RF, taking normal hold	Replace weight to LF, taking normal hold	2
9	LF back, turning to right	RF fwd, turning to right	1
10	RF almost closes to LF, still turning	LF almost closes to RF, still turning	2
11–14	Repeat Steps 9 and 10 twice, LRLR	Repeat Steps 9 and 10 twice, RLRL	1 2 1 2
15	LF back in Fallaway Position	RF back in Fallaway Position	1
16	Replace weight to RF in Promenade Position. Follow with Basic Side Step	Replace weight to LF in Promenade Position turning to face partner	2

8 Rhythm Movement

Commence in Normal Hold. Precede with Basic Side Step or Windmill.

	Man Weight on RF:	**Woman** Weight on LF:	**Timing**
1	LF to side	RF to side	1
2	RF closes to LF	LF closes to RF	2
3	Replace weight to LF, moving hips to left	Replace weight to RF, moving hips to right	1
4	Replace weight to RF, moving hips to right	Replace weight to LF, moving hips to left	2

Man	**Woman**	**Timing**
5–8 Repeat 1–4	Repeat 1–4	1 2 1 2

Follow with Basic Walk or Windmill.

9 Promenade Flick

Commence in Normal Hold.

	Man Weight on RF:	**Woman** Weight on LF:	**Timing**
1–4	Dance four steps of Basic Side Step LRLR	Dance four steps of Basic Side Step RLRL	1 2 1 2
5	LF forward in Promenade Position, turning ¼ to left, and flick RF from the floor at back to knee level, relaxing knees	RF forward in Promenade Position, turning ¼ to right, and flick LF from the floor at back to knee level, relaxing knees	1
6	RF forward in Promenade Position	LF forward in Promenade Position	2
7–8	Dance two steps of Basic Side Step, LF, turning to face partner	Dance two steps of Basic Side Step, RL, turning to face partner	1 2

Variation of Promenade Flick

1–4	Dance 4 steps of Basic Side Step	1 2 1 2
5–10	Dance Steps 5 and 6 three times, taking a short step on 5 and almost closing on 6	1 2 1 2 1 2
11–12	Dance 2 steps of Basic Side Step, turning to face partner	1 2
13–16	Follow with four steps of Basic Side Step	1 2 1 2

10 *Windmill*

Commence in Normal Hold.

Man Weight on RF:	**Woman** Weight on LF:	**Timing**
1–10 Precede with Steps 1–10 of Separation: on Steps 9 and 10 commence to raise arms		1 2 1 2 1 2 1 2 1 2
11–16 Both man and woman turn under raised arms; man to left, woman to right, taking six small steps forward for a complete turn		1 2 1 2 1 2
Man – LRLRLR	**Woman** – RLRLRL	
17–24 Repeat the turn, taking eight small steps forward		1 2 1 2
Man – LRLRLRLR	**Woman** – RLRLRLRL	1 2 1 2

Finish in Normal Hold. Follow with Basic Side Step or Rhythm Movement.

11 *Side Walk*

Commence in Normal Hold.

Man Weight on RF:	**Woman** Weight on LF:	**Timing**
1–4 Dance four steps of the Basic Side Step	Dance four steps of the Basic Side Step	1 2 1 2
5 LF to side	RF to side	1
6 RF closes to LF	LF closes to RF	and
7–8 Repeat 5 and 6 LR	Repeat 5 and 6 RL	2 and
9 LF to side (long step)	RF to side (long step)	1
10 RF closes to LF	LF closes to RF	2

Choreography

(a)   Basic Side Step.
Basic Side Step to Fallaway.
Left and Right Turns.
(b)   Basic Side Step.
Separation.
Promenade Flick.
Basic Side Step.
(c)   Basic Side Step.
Windmill.
Rhythm Movement.
(d)   Basic Side Step.
Separation with Arm Circle.
Basic Side Step.
(e)   Basic Walk turning to Left.
Separation.
Basic Side Step.
(f)   Basic Side Step.
Separation.
The Side Walk.
(g)   Basic Side Step.
Variation of Promenade Flick.
Left and Right Turns.

14

——— PASO DOBLE ———

The Paso Doble originated in Spain, the basic steps being essentially a type of march, or One-step, expressing the music which was composed to embody the colour and excitement of the bull ring.

Nevertheless, France was the country where the Paso Doble was developed in the ordinary social ballrooms. A simple version was danced in various parts of France but particularly in the southern region bordering on Spain. The French seemed to have a penchant for simplifying these dances and reducing them to a few rhythmic steps.

Several figures have French names. The first, and simplest figure, is named *sur place* and means 'on the spot'; *déplacement* means 'displacing, moving or transferring'; *huit* means the number 'eight' and the figure with this name has eight steps; *écart* comes from the word *écarter* and means 'to separate'; *appel* means 'a call' (the Matador's call to the bull). (G.W.)

The dance

Music

This is written in 2/4 time, one beat for each step, which should be well accented. The tempo is 60–62 bars per minute.

Footwork and hold

In the dancing, the man assumes the role of the matador and the woman represents his cape, therefore he should adopt a proud-looking and strong stance. The feet should be used firmly, with the knees very slightly flexed, but there should be full control over the muscles of the legs.

The footwork is heel flat for forward steps, ball flat for backward steps, ball of foot or ball flat for side steps and closing steps.

Any exceptions will be mentioned in the description of the figure.

The hold is closer than in Rumba and Samba, but is widened when dancing promenade figures.

Figures

In the Paso Doble many of the figures are progressive and therefore are danced moving around the room. Suggested alignments are given with all figures.

1   Sur Place

This is a series of four or eight steps, danced in Normal Hold, replacing the weight from one foot to the other, on the balls of the feet. The heels may be lowered lightly, and the knees are very slightly flexed. Sur Place may be danced with or without turn, each step taking one beat of music. The woman dances the normal opposite. The man will start with his RF, the woman with her LF.

2 Basic Movement

A series of four or eight forward or backward steps, danced in Normal Hold, on the balls of the feet. The heels may be lowered lightly and the knees are very slightly flexed. Basic Movement may be danced with or without turn, each step taking one beat of music. The woman dances the normal opposite. The man will start with his RF, the woman with her LF.

3 Appel

This is a firm step, danced on either foot, with foot flat and using a slight stamp. It is used to commence a number of figures.

4 Attack

Commence with Normal Hold. Precede with Sur Place.

	Man Facing LOD or diagonally wall, weight on LF:	**Woman** Backing LOD or diagonally wall, weight on RF:	**Timing**
1	Appel on RF	Appel on LF	1
2	LF forward	RF back	2
3	RF to side, turning ¼ turn to left between Steps 2 and 3	LF to side, turning ¼ turn to left	1
4	LF closes to RF	RF closes to LF	2

Note: The Attack may also be danced without turn.

Follow with Sur Place.

5   Chasses to Right and Left (with or without Elevation)

(a)   Chasses to Right

Commence in Normal Hold. Precede with Sur Place.

	Man Facing centre, weight on LF:	**Woman** Facing wall, weight on RF:	**Timing**
1	RF to side	LF to side	1
2	LF closes to RF	RF closes to LF	2
3	RF to side	LF to side	1
4	LF closes to RF	RF closes to LF	2

Note: The Chasses to Right may be commenced in any direction and may be curved Right or Left. They may be repeated.

Follow with Sur Place.

(b)   Chasses to Left

Commence in Normal Hold. Precede with Sur Place.

	Man Facing wall, weight on LF:	**Woman** Facing centre, weight on RF:	**Timing**
1	Appel on RF	Appel on LF	1
2	LF to side	RF to side	2
3	RF closes to LF	LF closes to RF	1
4	LF to side	RF to side	2

Note: The Chasses to Left may be commenced in any direction and can be curved to Right or Left. They may be repeated.

Follow with Sur Place.

(c) The Elevations

The Elevations are Chasses to Right or Left, danced with a change of height, either high on the toes with legs straight or with feet flat and knees slightly flexed.

(i)	2 Chasses up, 2 Chasses down	1 2 1 2
		1 2 1 2
(ii)	1 Chasse up, 1 Chasse down	1 2 1 2

6 Drag

Commence in Normal Hold. Precede with Sur Place.

	Man Facing centre, weight on LF:	**Woman** Facing wall, weight on RF:	**Timing**
1–4	Dance 2 Chasses to right with Elevation	Dance 2 Chasses to left with Elevation	1 2 1 2
5–8	2 Chasses to right; down	2 Chasses to left; down	1 2 1 2
9–12	Repeat Steps 1–4	Repeat Steps 1–4	1 2 1 2
13	RF to side, long step; down; Ball flat, bending right knee	LF to side, long step; down; Ball flat, bending left knee	1
14–16	Drag LF to RF, taking weight on LF on step 16, straightening right knee	Drag RF to LF, taking weight on RF on step 16, straightening left knee	2 1 2

Follow with Sur Place.

7 Promenade Link

Commence in Normal Hold. Precede with Sur Place.

	Man Facing LOD, weight on LF:	**Woman** Backing LOD, weight on RF:	**Timing**
1	Appel on RF	Appel on LF	1
2	LF to side in Promenade Position, heel flat, turning ⅛ to left between 1 and 2	RF to side in Promenade Position, heel flat, turning ⅛ to right between 1 and 2	2
3	RF forward and across in Promenade Position	LF forward in Promenade Position	1
4	LF closes to RF, turning ⅛ to left between 2 and 4	RF closes to LF, turning ⅜ to left between 3 and 4	2

Note: This figure may be danced in other directions.

Follow with Chasses to Right or Sur Place.

8 Separation

Commence in Normal Hold. Precede with Chasses to Right or Sur Place.

	Man Facing LOD, weight on LF:	**Woman** Backing LOD, weight on RF:	**Timing**
1	Appel on RF	Appel on LF	1
2	LF forward, commencing to lead woman to move away	RF back	2
3	RF closes to LF, leading woman to move away and releasing hold with right hand	LF back, releasing left hand	1

	Man	Woman	Timing
4	Sur Place on LF	RF closes to LF	2
5–8	4 Sur Place, RLRL, leading partner forward to Normal Position and Hold	4 Basic Movements forward, LRLR	1 2 1 2

Note: Steps 3–7 on balls of feet.

Elevation may be used on 4, gradually lowering over Steps 5–8. Follow with Sur Place or Chasses to Right.

9 Separation with Caping Walk

	Man	Woman	Timing
	Facing LOD, weight on LF:	Backing LOD, weight on RF:	
1–8	Commence in Normal Hold and precede this figure with the Separation, leading partner forward to right side over Steps 5–8, raising left arm and woman's right arm on 8		1 2 1 2 1 2 1 2
9–16	Man stands still (or marks time) for the next 8 counts, leading partner to pass from his right side to left side behind his back, to finish in front of him		1 2 1 2 1 2 1 2
		(Woman walks forward L R L R L R L R)	

Follow with Sur Place.

10 Huit (Cape)

Commence in Promenade Position, feet slightly apart. Precede with Sur Place, turning woman to Promenade Position, or 1–4 of Ecart.

	Man	Woman	Timing
	Facing diagonally wall, weight on LF:	Facing diagonally centre, weight on RF:	
1	RF forward and across in Promenade Position	LF forward and across in Promenade Position	1

	Man	**Woman**	**Timing**
2	LF closes to RF, turning ⅛ to right between 1 and 2 to face wall	RF to side, turning left; ball of foot	2
3–8	Sur Place RLRLRL; ball flat on each step	Replace weight to LF, ball flat, ¼ turn to left between 1 and 3	1
4		RF forward and across	2
5		LF to side, turning to right; ball of foot	1
6		Replace weight to RF; ball flat; ¼ turn to right between 4 and 6	2
7		LF forward towards partner	1
8		RF closes to LF, ⅛ turn to left between 7 and 8	2

Note: Man leads the woman to move to his left side on 2, to his right side on 5, towards him on 7 and to normal position on 8.

Follow with Sur Place or Chasses to Right.

11 Ecart (Fallaway Whisk) and Promenade Link to Right

Commence in Normal Hold. Precede with Sur Place.

	Man	**Woman**	**Timing**
	Facing wall, weight on LF:	Backing wall, weight on RF:	
1	Appel on RF	Appel on LF	1
2	LF forward	RF back	2

— **154** —

	Man	**Woman**	**Timing**
3	RF to side and slightly back in Fallaway; ball flat; turning ⅛ to left between 2 and 3	LF to side and slightly back in Fallaway; ball flat; turning ⅛ to right between 2 and 3	1
4	LF crosses behind RF in Fallaway; ball flat	RF crosses behind LF in Fallaway; ball flat	2
5	RF forward and across in Promenade Position	LF forward and across in Promenade Position	1
6	LF closes to Rf, turning ⅛ to right to face wall	RF closes to LF, turning ⅛ to left to face centre	2
7	RF to side	LF to side	1
8	LF closes to RF	RF closes to LF	2

Note: This figure may also be commenced facing diagonally wall or LOD.

Follow with Chasses to Right.

———————— Choreography ————————

(a) 4 Sur Place.
  The Drag.
  4 Sur Place.
(b) 4 Sur Place.
  Attack.
  2 Chasses to Right.
  4 Sur Place.
(c) Sur Place.
  Promenade Link.
  2 Chasses to Right.
  Sur Place.
(d) 4 Sur Place.
  Ecart and Promenade Link to Right.
  2 Chasses to Right.

— **155** —

(e)　4 Sur Place.
　　　1–4 of Ecart.
　　　Huit.
(f)　4 Sur Place.
　　　Promenade Link.
　　　2 Chasses to Right, turning to face LOD.
　　　Separation.
　　　Sur Place.
(g)　8 Sur Place.
　　　Separation with the Caping Walks.
　　　8 Sur Place.

ROCK 'N' ROLL

Fig. 15 Close hold for basic
movements.

Fig. 16 Double hold for basic
movements.

Fig. 17 Open hold as preparation for woman's under-arm turn.

Fig. 18 Open hold man's R hand holding woman's R hand as preparation for spins.

Fig. 19   Open hold man's L hand holding woman's L hand as preparation for man's turns.

Rock 'n' Roll is a dance with a fascinating history. Originating in Harlem it has developed a cosmopolitan character by embracing many types of foot patterns – spins, throws, jumps and lifts. The music has such enthusiasm, feeling and urgency that the dancer is given a series of rhythmic waves that makes the music seem to belong to that dancer, hence the individual interpretations. This type of music and dance is often the outcome of political or religious revolution.

This is certainly true of rock 'n' roll; because of the individual feeling of the dance, the steps and patterns suggested in this chapter are a guide only and when mastered will easily adapt to the dancer's own feelings.

The male dancer must at all times remember that his leads to the woman must be carefully calculated and rehearsed. The music is fast and the woman must understand clearly what she is intended to do.

The foot pattern timing remains consistent, but of course the arm patterns and shapes built on the foot pattern change very frequently.

Possibly the most used *shapes* are the under-arm turns and it is wise, in fact essential, that these are practised apart from the foot patterns to understand the need for soft but positive arm shapes, the use of the raising and lowering of the joined hands, the ability of the man to control the woman's turns and the sensitivity of the woman to accept the *leads* of the partner.

Suggested practice format

Man

Commence facing partner standing a little apart, weight on both feet, knees soft and pliable. Woman's Right Hand in man's Left Hand at approximately waist level. Relax arms so that they feel like a snake – no stiff joints:

1   Raise joined hands and prepare to pass the woman under the arch formed by joined hands (use bounce action in knees).

2   Lead her under the arch. She will turn about ¾ to her Right. At the completion of her turn lower the joined hands very positively to stabilise her and for the purpose of this rehearsal turn to face her approximately ¼ to Left, although this is not always how the turn will be.

3   To return her to original position raise joined hands, pass her under the arch and lower hands when her turn is completed. She should now have returned to commencing position.

Practise this action many, many times before adding the timing.

Bear in mind that the communication in Rock 'n' Roll, like Latin dancing, is in the hands and arms and they need as much rehearsal as the feet.

The man's under-arm turns should be rehearsed in the same way.

To achieve this *Talking with the hands* a further little exercise is very helpful. Have music playing, commence facing partner, weight on both feet, double hand hold approximately elbows distance apart.

1   Bounce knees in time to music. Very slightly sway to or lean to Left marking time in the hands and making sure that the partner understands the hand language. Now return to normal upright pose marking time in hands.

Practise to approximately a whole record using the knees at all times.

You are now ready to study the foot patterns of the Rock 'n' Roll.

As in other dances, only learn one figure or action at a time; rehearse it until it becomes natural, almost like breathing, and then tackle the next figure or step.

Figures

1 Rock Basic

Man
Commence in Closed or Open Facing Position, feet apart weight on RF:

		Amount of Turn	Count	Rhythm
1	LF sideways, small step, almost in place	Nil	1 2	S
2	Replace weight to RF	Nil	3 4	S
3	LF back, small step, leading the woman to step back on her RF		5	Q
4	Replace weight fwd to RF, leading the woman to replace weight fwd to her LF		6	Q
	Could be danced turning to the Left			

Woman
Commence in Closed or Open Facing Position, feet apart, weight on LF:

			Count	Rhythm
1	RF sideways, small step, almost in place	Nil	1 2	S
2	Replace weight to LF	Nil	3 4	S
3	RF back, small step		5	Q
4	Replace weight fwd on to LF		6	Q

2 Woman's Under Arm Turn to Right

Precede with Rock Basic.

Man
Commence in Closed or Open Facing Position, feet apart weight on RF:

		Amount of Turn	Count	Rhythm
1	LF fwd, raising joined hands and commence to turn woman to her R	Commence to turn L	1 2	S or QQ
2	RF to side, small step, close or almost close leading woman to complete her turn to R under joined hands. Lower joined hands at end of woman's turn	Complete ¼ turn L or no turn	3 4	S or QQ
3	LF back, small step, leading the woman to step back RF		5	Q
4	Replace weight fwd to RF leading woman to replace weight fwd to LF		6	Q
			1½ bars	

Woman
Commence in Closed or Open Facing Position, feet apart weight on LF:

			Count	Rhythm
1	RF fwd	Commence to turn R on Count 2	1 2	S or QQ
2	LF to side turning to R	Completing ¾ turn to R	3 4	S or QQ

		Amount of Turn	Count	Rhythm
3	RF back, small step		5	Q
4	Replace weight fwd to LF		6	Q
			1½ bars	

This could be followed by Change of Places L to R; Push Spin; Change of Hands Behind back; or Man's Under Arm Turn.

3 Woman's Under Arm Turn to Left

Precede with any Rock Basic action, Woman's Under Arm Turn to Right or push spin.

Man
Commence in Open Facing Position or woman on man's L Side at right angles, feet apart, weight on RF:

		Amount of Turn	Count	Rhythm
1	LF in place, raising joined hands and commence to turn woman to her Left	Commence to turn Right	1 2	S or QQ
2	RF to side, small step, almost close, leading woman to complete her turn to L under joined hands. Lower joined hands at end of woman's turn	Completing ¼ turn to R or no turn	3 4	S or QQ
3	LF back, small step, leading the woman to step back on RF		5	Q

		Amount of Turn	**Count**	**Rhythm**
4	Replace weight fwd to RF, leading the woman to replace weight fwd to LF		6	Q

				1½ bars

Woman

Commence in Open Facing Position, feet apart, weight on LF:

1	RF fwd	Commence to turn L on Count 2	1 2	S or QQ
2	LF back	Completing ¾ turn to L	3 4	S or QQ
3	RF back (small step)		5	Q
4	Replace weight fwd to LF		6	Q

				1½ bars

4 Man's Under Arm Turn to Right

Precede with any figure which ends in Open Facing Position.

Man

Commence in Open Facing Position, feet apart, weight on RF:

		Amount of Turn	**Count**	**Rhythm**
1	LF fwd turning sharply to R, raising joined hands	Commence to turn R	1 2	S or QQ

		Amount of Turn	Count	Rhythm
2	RF to side, lowering joined hands at the end of turn	Completing 1 full turn Right	3 4	S or QQ
3	LF back small step, leading the woman to step back RF		5	Q
4	Replace weight fwd to RF, leading the woman to replace weight fwd to LF		6	Q
			1½ bars	

Woman

The woman will dance basic action in place (no turn). Count and Rhythm will depend on man's action.

Any suitable figure can follow this.

5 Man's Under Arm Turn to Left

This may be danced with two different amounts of turn:

1   Foot positions and amount of turn as for Change of Hands Behind Back. Man will turn L under joined hands.

2   Man will dance one complete turn to L. Woman will dance Basic in place.

6 Additional Under Arm Turn

Woman's Under Arm Turns to R and L may also be danced with Right to Right hand hold.

Woman's Under Arm Turn to L, R hand to R hand hold may also be danced to pass behind man's back. Amount of turn as follows:

1 Man ¼ turn to L raising joined hands and leading the woman to turn ¾ to L, passing behind man's back to end on his L side. Man's R arm will now be behind his back.

  Woman will make ½ turn to L, ending in tandem position.

This can be followed by the Shoulder Spin or the Umbrella (not included in this).

7 Push Spin to Right and Left

Commence in Open Facing Position, feet apart, weight on LF:

		Amount of Turn	Count	Rhythm
1	RF fwd, woman leaning slightly against man's hand, turning to R on Count 2	Spin on RF Turn to R Count 2	1 2	S
2	LF back small step	Completing 1 full turn to R	3 4	S
3	RF back small step		5	Q
4	Replace weight fwd to LF		6	Q
			1½ bars	

Note: Man will dance Basic Action usually with no turn, bracing joined hands and leading the woman to turn on Count 2.

The Push Spin can be led by the man with either his L or R hand and may be danced with or without hold.

The man may also dance a Push Spin with the same action as the woman, using LF first and spinning to the L.

8 Alternative Basic Action

(a) Tap Basic

Man
Commence in Closed or Open Facing Position, feet apart weight on RF:

		Amount of Turn	Count	Rhythm
1	Tap LF to side (part weight)	Nil	1	Q
2	Place full weight on to LF		2	Q
3	Tap RF to side (part weight)		3	Q
4	Place full weight on to RF		4	Q
5	LF back, small step, leading woman to step back RF		5	Q
6	Replace weight fwd to RF, leading woman to replace weight fwd to LF		6	Q

(b) Advanced Methods Of Tap Basic

1	Hop on RF, tap LF to side (strong sway to R)		a 1	Q
2	Slip RF towards LF, lifting L knee		&	&
3	Place full weight on to LF		2	Q
4	Hop on LF. Tap RF to side (strong sway to L)		a 3	Q

		Amount of Turn	Count	Rhythm
5	Slip LF towards RF, lifting R knee		&	&
6	Place full weight on to RF		4	Q
7	Tap heel of LF fwd		5	Q
8	LF back (part weight)		&	&
9	Replace full weight to RF		6	Q

Note: Steps 7–9 may also be danced as a Flick Ball Change action.

(c) Flick Basic

Man

Commence in Open Facing Position, feet apart weight on RF:

		Amount of Turn	Count	Rhythm
1	Hop on RF, Flick LF fwd	Nil	a 1	Q
2	Hop on RF, close LF to RF		a 2	Q
3	Hop on LF, Flick RF fwd		a 3	Q
4	Hop on LF, close RF to LF		a 4	Q
5	LF back, small step, leading woman to step back RF		5	Q
6	Replace weight fwd to RF, leading woman to replace weight fwd to LF		6	Q

Choreography

Basic in Place.
Woman's Under Arm Turn to her R.
Woman's Under Arm Turn to her L.
Basic in Place (L Hand hold only).
Man's Under Arm Turn to his L (½ turn).
Basic In Place.
Man's Under Arm Turn to his R.
Basic in place.
Woman's Push Spin to her R.
Repeat.

Additional Under Arm Turns can be used at any point with the above figures.

DISCO/FREESTYLE DANCES

Introduction

Disco and freestyle dancing can be likened to the rhythmic movement danced by the natives of Africa in which people expressed, in dance form, their feelings of happiness, sorrow, hate, and even war, to their own music provided by instruments made from the bark of trees, animal skins, tuberous plants, and so on. In this form of dance one does not need a partner and the personal interpretation of the music usually reflects the mood of the dancer. However, a few basic movements are a great help, and a study of the basic Disco steps will give the dancer a start, then the body movement and arm and hip actions can be added. Arm movements often reflect day to day actions, such as serving at tennis, skating, swimming, answering the telephone, and so on.

There is a tremendous feeling of rhythmic exhilaration in being able to dance completely freely, uninhibited and unencumbered by a partner. Nevertheless many discotheques play only this type of music, often very loud, so if you visit this type of dancing venue, you must equip yourself with the general style of dancing. Dancing schools usually cover what are known as *Line Dances* where the pupils are taught a small sequence, usually to 4, 6 or 8 bars of music. The steps are Disco steps but in a set sequence to a particular record. This is a very relaxed way to learn rhythm and feeling to music, similar to limbering in Jazz or classical ballet. Many of the actual foot patterns taught are taken from dances like the Samba, Cha Cha Cha and Jive, and so help to guide the dancer into the natural feeling for these figures. A line dance can often be adapted to a 'facing partner' dance by changing the step so that the couple are dancing on opposite feet, and not on the same foot as each other.   (P.S.)

The dance

Music

Chart music changes from month to month. The music writers, groups and musicians are continually composing new types of music and new combinations of sound, and the dancing teachers try to interpret this music in dance form. These trends may only last a short time but are fun while they last. The line dances described below can be danced to any chart music of medium to fast tempo.

Footwork

The first and most important part of freestyle dancing is to develop rhythmic feeling in the legs and body before attempting steps. Work on the following exercises – often called *Popcorn* – and practise them to music.

———— Initial exercise ————

Commence with feet together, your knees softly flexed (not bent); bounce your knees down and up, without moving your feet and counting *One, two, one two* (single action). Then gradually introduce a double bounce by counting *a one, a two, a one, a two*.

Allow the arms to swing softly, relax your shoulders and gradually let the body turn right and left as the knees bounce, without moving your feet. After rehearsing this to music for some time, gradually bring the right arm almost to the right ear in rhythm as though answering the telephone and then as the arm swings down lift up the left arm. This can be done to produce the effect of serving at tennis, milking a cow and so on, but must be in rhythm, using the knees continuously to the music. All parts of the body should feel relaxed and ready to be used to music at any time; for instance, a slight shoulder shake or an arm action might be part of a step and that part of the body must be ready. Part of the freestyle dance can be done in this way of using rhythmic arm and body movements and not foot movements. However, it is exhilarating to have some step patterns as well, so here are some simple ones that can be used in any order. Most Disco dancers develop just two or three foot patterns and alternate and repeat these according to the feeling of the music.

Disco and freestyle can be danced as 'solo' or couple dances or in a circle type pattern with a number of friends all doing their 'own thing'.

Man and Woman	**Timing**
Commence with weight on RF (direction not important)	

1	Step on to LF in place, bouncing knees down	a 1
2	Point RF forward and slightly to R on heel or toe, without weight, using slight body turn to R and allowing arms to swing into a soft shape with body. Knees will slightly straighten	a 2
3	Almost close RF to LF bouncing knees down	a 1
4	Point LF forward and slightly to L on heel or toe, without weight, using slight body turn to L allowing arms to swing into a soft shape with body. Knees will slightly straighten	a 2

Repeat this over and over again. An easy way to master the knee action is to say *bend* on the closing step and *straight* on the pointing step and sing it in rhythm – *bend, straight, bend, straight,* and so on.

Some dancers prefer to commence with the *straight* action as the feet close and the *bend* as the foot is pointed, but this is a personal thing which can develop when the dancer knows the basic step.

———————— Side Basic ————————

		Timing
1	LF to side small step	a 1
2	Close RF to LF without weight with slight body turn to R	a 2
3	RF side small step. Return body to starting position.	a 1
4	Close LF to RF without weight, with slight body turn to L	a 2

Note: The closing step without weight will end with the heel of the LF (or RF) approximately to the instep of the supporting foot with the toe turned out.

The arms can be used by turning the elbows in towards the body on the *a 2* count and raising the hands slightly, but keep the action low and subtle.

—————— Freestyle Chasse ——————

		Timing
1	LF to side (small step)	a 1
2	RF almost closes to LF	a 2
3	LF to side small step	a 3
4	Close RF to LF without weight, with slight body turn to R	a 4

Note: The closing step should be danced as in the Side Basic and the arms can be used in the same way.

Repeat these four steps starting with RF turning body slightly L on fourth Step.

The three step patterns described can be used in any order and each are repeated as often as desired. The joy of beat is the feeling of being able to change step when you feel like it.

The following are three Line dances which are a disciplined form of disco dancing – several people dancing the same routine at the same time. This can be great fun at a party or dance.

————————— The Slosh —————————

This is the easiest and most popular Line disco dance for beginners. It is danced in lines – man and woman using the same foot.

Music

Medium tempo strong beat chart music.

Commence facing the wall with weight on RF.

Timing

Fig. 1

1	LF to side	1
2	RF closes, or almost closes, to LF	2
3	LF to side	3
4	Kick RF across LF	
	(Say *1 2 3 Kick*)	4

Fig. 2 Repeat Fig. 1 to Right, starting with RF
(Say *1 2 3 Kick*)   1 2 3 4

Fig. 3 Repeat Fig. 1 (Say *1 2 3 Kick*)   1 2 3 4

Fig. 4 Repeat Fig. 2 but kick LF up behind RF and touch
L heel with R hand (Say *1 2 3 Kick*)   1 2 3 4

Fig. 5 Commencing to turn to R
Place LF down with weight   1
Lift RF off floor in front, bending knee and
slapping R knee with R hand   2
Place RF down with weight   3
Lift LF off floor in front with knee high and clap
hands under L knee   4
(Say *step – lift – step – clap*)
Make a ¼ turn to right on the four steps.

Commence dance again from this new
alignment.

Repeat each sequence on a new line having made ¼ turn to R on each
one.

—————————— **The Split** ——————————

A Line dance to slow or reggae-type music. Commence in lines, weight on RF

		Timing
Fig. 1	LF to side	1
	Almost close RF to LF	2
	LF to side	3
	Tap RF to LF without weight	4
	(*Side – close – side Tap*)	
Fig. 2	Repeat these four steps starting with RF but when tapping LF to RF bend knees ready for jump action	1 2 3 4
	(*Side – close – side Tap*)	
Fig. 3	(Split) With a light jumping action split feet apart then bring them together with LF crossed in front of RF	1 2
Fig. 4	Keeping knees together rock on to RF in place and then on to LF in place. Finish with weight on LF	3 4
Fig. 5	Kick RF forward	1
	Cross RF in front of LF and turn a ¼ to the L	2
	Place LF to side small step	3
	Close RF to LF	4

Repeat this dance from the beginning on new alignment.

A little energetic but great fun. The music needs to be slightly slower than the normal beat – the Reggae-type music is ideal.

Dizzy

Can be used as a Line dance or facing partner. When danced facing partner normal opposite foot is used. The music should have a good medium tempo.

Man

Commence facing partner, weight on LF.

		Timing
Fig. 1	Point RF to R side without weight	1
	Close RF to LF without weight	2
	Point RF to R side without weight	3
	Close RF to LF with weight	4
	Repeat these four steps starting with LF pointing to side	1 2 3 4
Fig. 2	As Fig. 1, but point RF slightly back instead of to side and look towards it	1 2 3 4
	Repeat these four steps but starting with LF pointing slightly back	1 2 3 4
Fig. 3	Lift RF off floor in front with knee high and touch knee with left elbow	1
	Place RF down without weight	2
	Lift RF off floor again and touch knee with left elbow	3
	Place RF down with weight	4
	Now repeat these four steps lifting LF off floor and touching knee with R elbow	1 2 3 4
Fig. 4	Turn a ¼ to R then RF forward	1
	LF closes towards R	2
	RF forward and at end of step turn a ½ to L	3
	Draw LF towards RF without weight, toe turned out	4
	(This figure can be likened to a skating action)	

<table>
<tr><td></td><td>**Timing**</td></tr>
</table>

Repeat these four steps starting with LF making
no turn on first step – end ready to start dance
again.

1 2 3 4

Chant in rhythm:– *Point* *2 3 4*
                  Point *2 3 4*
                  Point *2 3 4*
                  Back   *2 3 4*
                  Back   *2 3 4*
                  Lift   *2 3 4*
                  Lift   *2 3 4*
                  Skate *2 3 4*
                  Skate *2 3 4*
                  Start again.

This dance is fun at parties if danced in a circle – in which case all are on
same foot.

———————— Brother Louie ————————

Music

It is best to use strong, medium tempo music.

Walks forward and back

Start with weight on LF.

	Timing
RF fwd	1
LF fwd	2
RF fwd	3
LF fwd	4

	Timing
RF Back	1
LF Back	2
RF Back	3
LF Back	4

Repeat using a loose arm swing on the forward steps and finger shapes on backward steps.

Charleston Points

1	Swing RF fwd	1
2	Swing RF Back	2
3	Swing RF fwd	
4	Place RF to side and stand on it with full weight	4
	Repeat this figure with LF	1 2 3 4

Chasses to Right and Left with hand clap

1	RF to side	1
2	LF closes to RF	2
3	RF to side	3
4	LF crosses loosely behind RF without weight with slight body bend to left and low hand clap	4
1	LF to side	1
2	RF closes to LF	2
3	LF to side	3
4	RF crosses loosely behind LF without weight and slight body bend to Left and low hand clap.	

Weight is now on LF and RF is free to commence again with Step 1.

Each figure can be repeated according to the feelings of the dancer and the phrasing of the music.

ORGANISATIONS WORLDWIDE

Australia: Australian Dancing Board, 49 Links Road, Ardross 6153; Federal Association of Teachers of Dancing, 161 Castlereah Street, Sydney.

Austria: Verband der Tanzlehrer Osterreichs, Ferenc Polai, Reichenauerstrasse 99, A-6020, Innsbruck.

Belgium: Buldo UBPDM, Vogelenzang 21, B2150 Borsbeek

Canada: Canadian Dance Teachers' Association, Patrick Bovaird, 94 Boulevard Lavesque, Pont Viau, Laval, Quebec H7G 1C1.

Denmark: Danselaerer Organisationernes Forening, Jorgen Christensen, Frederiksvaerksgade 43 A, 3400 Hillerod.

Estonia: Estonian Association of Teachers of Dancing, Box 3545, 200090 Tallinn.

Finland: Suomen Tanssinopettajain Liitto r.y., Voudink Marko Ala-Ketola, Satulavyontie 5, 90540 OULU.

France: Academie des Maitres de Danse de France, Rene Barsi, 22 Rue Victor Hugo, 93110 Montreuil.

Germany: ADTV President, Monchengang 7–9, 4600 Dortmund.

Great Britain: British Council of Ballroom Dancing, Mary Edwards, 87 Parkhurst Road, Holloway, London N7 0LP.

Greece: President NDTAGB & L, 25th Martiou Str. 5, Peristeri 12100, Athens.

Holland: Federatie Dansleraren Orgaisaties, Fred Bijster, J B Weg 6, 7991 RG Dwingeloo & David Simon, Sinjeur Semeyn Straat, 1183 Ld Amstelveen.

Hong Kong: Hong Kong Ballroom Dancing Council, No 10 Jubilee Street, Room 502, Central HK.

Hungary: CHPDT Secretary, H-112 Budapest, Menyecska u. 37

Iceland: Dansrao Islands, Heidar R'Astvaldsson, Box 5048, Reykjavik.

Indonesia: Indonesian Council of Ballroom Dancing, Sunarjati Chen, 5 JLN K H Wahid Hasyim, Jakarta 10340.

Ireland: All Ireland Board of Ballroom Dancing, James Byrne, 7 Muckross Park, Dublin 12.

Italy: Consiglio Italiano Del Ballo, Adalberto Dell'Orto, Via C Monteverdi 10, Ponteterra, 46018 Sabbionetta.

Japan: Nippon League of Competitive Ballroom Dancing, Ishikawa 1st Building, Room 203, 20–1 Misaki-cho 2-chome, Chiyoda-ku, Tokyo 101.

Korea: Chairman, Korean National Council of Ballroom Dancing, 3F Youngsin Bldg, 18, 5-Ga Youngdungpo-Dong, Youngdungpo-Gu, Seoul.

Malaysia: Malaysian Dancers' Association, Chan Seang Teik, 14 Jesselton Road, Penang.

New Zealand: New Zealand Council of Ballroom Dancing, Sherrall Macown, PO Box 37–342, Parnell, Auckland.

Norway: Norges Danselaerer-Forbund, Svein Rotvold, Karisveien 178, 2013 Skjetten.

Poland: Polish Professional Dance Association, 84–230 Rumia ul Kamienna 5.

Scotland: Scottish Dance Teachers' Alliance, Johnny Stewart, 6 Richmond Road, Bishopbriggs, Glasgow G64 3HR.

Singapore: Singapore Ballroom Dance Teachers' Association, PO Box 0265, Bras Basah, Singapore 0265.

South Africa: South African Dance Teachers' Association, Gloria Fish, PO Box 75677, Gardenview 2047.

Spain: Asociaciòn Española de Profesores de Bailes de Salon, Mariona Cortes, Gran de Gracia 51, 08012 Barcelona.

Sri Lanka: Sri Lanka Association of Ballroom Dancing Professionals, No 7 Charles Circus, Colombo 3.

Sweden: Sveriges Dans Pedagogers Riksforbund, Nygatan 46, 702 11 Orebro.

Switzerland: Schweizer Organisation der Berufstanslehrer, Willy F Kummer, Seestrasse 93, CH-8820 Waedenswil.

Taiwan: ROC Council of Ballroom Dancing, 10F-2, 46 Section 2, San Ming Road, Taichung.

Thailand: Thailand Association of Teachers of Dancing, Priyabhan Bunyavibul, 240/7-242 New City Bldg, 3rd Floor, Siam Square, Sol 2 Phatumwan, Bangkok 10500.

United States: National Dance Council of America, 2 Alhambra Plaza #12, Coral Gables, Florida.

USSR: USSR Music Society/Association of Professional Ballroom Dancers and Teachers, Gertsen Str. 14/2, 103009 Moscow and Novatorov Str. 26–52 117421 Moscow.

Yugoslavia: Zdruzenje plesnih uciteljew Slovenije-Jugoslavija (ZPUS), Boris Oblak, Ruska 11, 61000, Ljubljana.